when
CHRIST
returns

when CHRIST returns

CHARLES SPURGEON

Whitaker House

WHEN CHRIST RETURNS

ISBN: 0-88368-433-0
Printed in the United States of America
Copyright © 1997 by Whitaker House

Whitaker House
30 Hunt Valley Circle
New Kensington, PA 15068

4 5 6 7 8 9 10 11 12 / 07 06 05 04 03 02

Contents

Chapter One

An Awful Premonition

Verily I say unto you, There be some standing here, which shall not taste of death, till they see the Son of man coming in his kingdom.
—Matthew 16:28

I confess that I have frequently read this verse with only a vague sense of its poignancy and have passed over it rapidly because I have not understood it clearly. Although I am well acquainted with the usual interpretations, none of them has ever really satisfied me. This text seems to arouse the reader's surprise without suggesting a simple, obvious meaning. Bible commentators have thus invented explanations and offered suggestions that are widely divergent, but all are equally obscure and improbable.

Lately, however, in reading a volume of sermons by Bishop Horsley, I have met with an altogether new view of the passage, which I firmly believe to be the correct one. Though I do not suppose I will be able to convince all of you of this interpretation, yet I will do my best to elicit from our text the terrible charge that I believe the Savior has left here on record.

With His own cross in mind, Jesus had just admonished His disciples to steadfastness and appealed to them to take up their crosses and follow Him at any sacrifice, which He followed with a portrayal of the inestimable value of the soul and the horror of a soul being lost. (See Matthew 16:24–26.) The full force of that doom was (and is) impossible to comprehend until He *"shall come in the glory of his Father with his angels"* (Matthew 16:27). Then He stopped, looked on some of the company, and said something like this: "Certain people are standing here who will never taste of death until they see the Son of Man coming in His kingdom."

Now, what did He mean by this? Obviously, it is either a marvelous promise to some who were His disciples indeed, or else it is a portent of woe to others who would die in their sins. How do the popular interpretations of our learned commentators view this statement of our Lord?

Some say it refers to the Transfiguration. It certainly is remarkable that the account of the Transfiguration immediately follows this verse both in Mark and in Luke, as well as in this record of Matthew. However, can you for a moment convince yourself to believe that Christ was describing His Transfiguration when He spoke of *"the Son of man coming in his kingdom"*? Can you see any connection between the Transfiguration and the preceding verse that says,

> [27] *For the Son of man shall come in the glory of his Father with his angels; and then he shall reward every man according to his works.* (Matthew 16:27)

I grant you that Christ was in His glory on Mount Tabor, but He did not *"reward every man according to his works"* there. Neither is it at all fair to call that a "coming of the Son of Man." He did not *"come"* on Mount Tabor because He was already on earth. It is a misuse of language to construe that into an advent.

Besides, what would be the reason for such a solemn introduction as *"Verily I say unto you"*? Does it not raise expectations merely to cause disappointment, if He intended to say no more than this: *"There be some standing here, which shall not taste of death, till they see'* Me

9

transfigured"? That scene took place only six days later. The next verse tells you so.

> [1] *And after six days Jesus taketh Peter, James, and John his brother, and bringeth them up into an high mountain apart.*
> (Matthew 17:1)

You see, the majesty of the prediction, which carries our thoughts forward to the last days of the world's history, makes us shrink from accepting an immediate fulfillment of it. Thus, I cannot imagine that the Transfiguration is in the slightest degree referred to here. Further, I do not think that anyone would have thought of such a thing unless he had been confused and utterly perplexed in searching for an explanation.

Although it seems almost incredible, some learned scholars endorse this view. Moreover, they say that it also refers to the descent of the Holy Spirit. I am staggered at this thought. I cannot think how any man could find an analogy with Pentecost in the context here. Pentecost took place six months after this event. I really cannot comprehend why Jesus Christ would say, "Truly I say unto you, there are some standing here who will live six months." It seems to me that my Master did not waste people's time by speaking such inanities.

Who, reading this passage, can think it has any reference to the descent of the Holy Spirit?

> [27] *For the Son of man shall come in the glory of his Father with his angels; and then he shall reward every man according to his works.* (Matthew 16:27)

Did Christ come at Pentecost in the glory of His Father? Were there any angels accompanying Him at that time? Did He *"reward every man according to his works"* then? Scarcely can the descent of the Holy Spirit or the appearance of *"cloven tongues like as of fire"* (Acts 2:3) be called *"the Son of man* [coming] *in the glory of his Father with his angels* [to] *reward every man according to his works"* without a gross misuse of our language or a strange violation of symbolic imagery.

Both of these theories that I have mentioned are now rejected as unsatisfactory by those modern students who have most carefully studied the subject. However, a third explanation still holds its ground and is currently received, though I believe it to be quite as far from the truth as the others.

Carefully read through the sixteenth chapter of Matthew, and you will find nothing about the siege of Jerusalem there. Yet, this is the interpretation that finds favor at present.

According to those who hold this view, Christ was referring to the time when Jerusalem would be destroyed by the Romans. But, why would Jesus have said that some who were standing there would be alive then? Nothing could be more foreign to the entire scope of Christ's narrative or the gospel accounts. There is not the slightest shadow of reference to the siege of Jerusalem. The coming of the Son of Man is spoken of here: *"in the glory of his Father with his angels;* [when] *he shall reward every man according to his works."*

Whenever Jesus spoke of the coming siege of Jerusalem, He was accustomed to saying, *"Verily I say unto you, This generation shall not pass, till all these things be fulfilled"* (Matthew 24:34). Never, however, did He single out a select few and say to them, *"'Verily I say unto you, There be some standing here, which shall not taste of death,'* until the city of Jerusalem is besieged and destroyed."

If a child were to read this passage, I know what he would think it meant: he would suppose Jesus Christ is to come again to the earth, and there were some standing there who would not taste of death until really and literally He did so. This, I believe, is the plain meaning.

"Well," I hear someone saying, "I am surprised. Do you think, then, that this refers to

the apostle John?" No, by no means. The fable
that John was to live until Christ came again
was current in early New Testament times,
you know. However, John himself repudiated
it, for at the end of his gospel, he said,

> [23] *Then went this saying abroad among the
> brethren, that that disciple should not die:
> yet Jesus said not unto him, He shall not
> die; but, if I will that he tarry till I come,
> what is that to thee?*
> (John 21:23, emphasis added)

This, you see, was setting forth a hypothetical
case, and in no sense was it the language of
prediction.

Now, beloved, if you are so far convinced
of the unreasonableness of each of these theories to resolve the difficulty of interpretation, I
hope that you are in readiness for the explanation that appears to me to harmonize with
every aspect of the text. I believe the *"coming"*
referred to in our text is the coming of the Son
of God to judge at the last great and terrible
Day, when He will judge all and separate the
wicked from among the righteous.

The next question is, Of whom were the
words spoken? Are we warranted in supposing
that our Lord intended this sentence as a gracious promise or a kindly expectation that He

wanted to kindle in the hearts of His disciples? I trust not. To me it appears to have absolutely no reference to any man who ever had grace in his soul. Such language is far more applicable to the ungodly than to the wicked. The sentence may well have been aimed directly at those followers who would defect from the faith, grasp at the world, endeavor to save their lives but really lose them, and barter their souls.

A True Taste of Death

At the glorious appearing of Christ, there are some who will taste death, but will they be the righteous? Surely, my dear friends, when Christ comes, the righteous will not die. They will be caught up with the Lord in the air. His coming will be the signal for the resurrection of all His saints.

But, at the time of His return, the men who have been without God, without Christ, will begin for the first time to *"taste of death."* They will have passed the first stage of dissolution when their souls abandon their bodies, but they will have never known the *"taste of death."* Until Christ's return, they will not have truly known its tremendous bitterness and its awful horror. They will never drink the wormwood and the gall, to really *"taste of death,"* until that time. This tasting of death may be explained, and I believe it is to be explained, as a reference to the second death of which men will not taste until the Lord comes again.

What a dreadful sentence that was when the Savior said (perhaps singling out Judas as He spoke), "Truly I say unto you, there are some who are standing here who will never know what that dreadful word *death* really means until the Lord comes again. You think that if you save your lives, you escape from death. Alas, you do not know what death means! The demise of the body is but a mere prelude to the perdition of the soul. The grave is but the porch of death. You will never understand the full meaning of that terrible word until the Lord comes."

This can have no reference to the saints, because in the gospel of John, you find this passage:

> [51] *Verily, verily, I say unto you, If a man keep my saying, he shall never see death.*
> [52] *Then said the Jews unto him, Now we know that thou hast a devil. Abraham is dead, and the prophets; and thou sayest, If a man keep my saying, he shall never taste of death.*   (John 8:51–52)

No righteous man, therefore, can ever *"taste of death."* Yes, he will fall into that deep, oblivious sleep during which the body sees corruption, but that is another experience, very different from the bitter cup referred to as a *"taste of death."* When the Holy Spirit wanted to use an expression to set forth the equivalent for divine wrath, what wording was used? *"Jesus, who was made a little lower than the angels for suffering of death...by the grace of God should taste death for every man"* (Hebrews 2:9).

The expression "to taste of death" means the reception of the true, essential death that kills both the body and the soul in hell forever. The Savior said, *"Verily I say unto you, There be some standing here, which shall not taste of death, till they see the Son of man coming in his kingdom."* If this is the meaning (and I hold that it is in keeping with the context), it explains the verse, sets forth the reason why Christ invoked breathless attention with the word *verily,* answers both the grammar and the rhetoric, and will not be moved by any argument that I have ever heard. And if so, what amazing indictments are contained in this text! May the Holy Spirit deeply affect our hearts and cause our souls to thrill with its solemnity.

What thoughts this idea stirs up! Compared with the doom that will be inflicted upon the ungodly at Christ's return, the death of the physical body is nothing. Further, compared with the doom of the wicked at His return, even the torment of souls in a separate state is scarcely anything. The startling question then arises: Are there any reading this who will have to taste of death when the Lord comes?

Comparing Physical Death and Final Doom

The sinner's death is only a faint fore-shadowing of the sinner's doom at the coming of the Son of Man in His glory. Let me endeavor to show the contrast.

In Regard to Time

We can only make a little comparison between the two as to time. Many men meet with death so suddenly that it can scarcely involve any pain to them. Perhaps they are crushed by machinery, or a shot sends them to find a grave upon the battlefield, or they are poisoned with a quick-acting toxin. Even if they are upon the bed of sickness for hours, days, weeks, or months, yet the real work of dying is short. It is a weary sort of living, rather than an actual process of dying, while hope lingers, though only in fitful dreams. Dying is but the work of a moment. If it is said to last for hours, yet the hours are brief. Misery may count them long, but with what swift wings do they fly. To die, to fall asleep, to suffer, may seem endless, yet to pass away from the land of the living into the realm of shadows takes only a moment!

However, the doom that is to be brought upon the wicked when Christ comes is a death that never dies. Here is a heart that palpitates with eternal misery. Here is an eye that is never clouded over by the kind finger of generous forgetfulness. Here is a body that never will be stiffened in apathy, never will be laid quietly in the grave, rid of sharp pains, wearying disease, and lingering wretchedness. To die, you say, is nature's kind release, because it brings ease. To a man, death becomes a farewell to his woes and griefs—for this world at least.

Yet, there will be no ease, no rest, no pause in the destination of impenitent souls. *"Depart from me, ye cursed"* (Matthew 25:41) will ever ring along the endless aisles of eternity. The thunderbolt of that tremendous word will follow the sinner in his perpetual flight from the presence of God. From its deadly influence he will never be able to escape—no, never. A million years will not make any more difference to the duration of his agony than a cup of water taken from the sea would change

18

the volume of the ocean. When a million years have rolled their fiery orbits over his poor, tormented head, he will be no nearer to the end than he was at first.

Talk about physical death! I might even portray it as an angel of mercy when I compare it to the terrors of the wrath to come. Soon come, soon gone, is death. That sharp scythe gives only one cut, and down falls the flower that withers in the heat of the sun. But, who can measure the wounds of eternity, who can fathom the depths of its gashes? When eternity wields the whip, how dreadfully it falls! When eternity grasps the sword, how deep is the wounding and how terrible the killing!

> To linger in eternal pain,
> Yet death for ever fly.

You are afraid of death, sinner; you are afraid of death. However, were you wise, you would be ten thousand times ten thousand times more afraid of the Second Coming and the Judgment of the Son of Man.

As to Loss

Regarding loss, there is no comparison. When a sinner dies, it is not tasting death in its true sense, for what does he lose? He loses wife and children and friends. He loses all his hearty meat and his sweet desserts. Where are his violin and his lute now? Where are the merry dances and the joyful company? For him there is no more pleasant landscape or gliding stream. For him the light of the sun by day or the light of the moon and stars by night shines no more. At one stroke, he has lost every comfort and every hope. The loss, however, as far as physical death is concerned, is but a loss of earthly things, the loss of material, temporary comforts. It is wretched enough to lose these, but he might put up with that kind of loss.

Nevertheless, let your imagination follow me, faint as my power is to describe the everlasting and infinite loss of the man who is found impenitent at the last great Judgment Day. What does he lose then? The harps of heaven and the songs thereof, the joys of God's presence and the light thereof, the jasper sea and the gates of pearl. He has lost peace and immorality and the crown of life.

Moreover, he has lost all hope. When a man has lost that, what remains for him? His spirit sinks into a terrible depression, more frightening than a madman ever knew in his wildest moods of grief. Never to recover itself, his soul sinks into the depths of dark despair, where not a ray of hope can ever reach him.

Lost to God, lost to heaven, lost to time, lost to the preaching of the Gospel, lost to the invitation of mercy, lost to the prayers of the gracious, lost to the mercy seat, lost to the blood of sprinkling, lost to all hope of every sort— lost, lost, forever lost! Compared with this loss, the losses of death are nothing. Thus, the Savior said that lost souls will not even *"taste of death"* until He comes and they receive their sentences.

Concerning Terror

Neither does death bear any comparison with the Judgment concerning terror. I do not like to describe the terrors of the deathbeds of unawakened men. Some, you know, glide gently into their graves. In fact, it is often the mark of the wicked that they have no troubles in dying, but their strength stays firm. They are not distraught as other men are. Like sheep they are laid in the grave. Yet, a peaceful death is no sign of grace. Some of the worst men have died with smiles on their faces, only to have them exchanged for eternal weeping.

However, other men of exquisite sensitivities, educated men, cannot seem to die like brute animals do. They have intense fears and terrors when they are on their deathbeds.

Many an atheist has cried out to God when he was experiencing the pangs of death. Many an infidel, who previously bragged and spoke high things against God, has found his cheek turn pale and his throat grow hoarse when he has come to the throes of death. Like the mariner, the boldest man in the great storm of death reels and staggers like a drunkard and is at his wit's end, because he finds that it is no child's play to die.

I try sometimes to picture that hour when we will be propped up in bed, or perhaps lying down with pillows all around us, being diligently watched. As loved ones hush their footfalls and gaze anxiously on, there is a whisper that the solemn time has come. Then there is a grappling of the strong man with one stronger than he. Oh, what must it be to die without a Savior—to die in the dark without a light except the lurid glare of the wrath to come!

Horrors there are, indeed, around the deathbed of the wicked, but these are hardly anything compared with the terrors of the Day of Judgment. When the sinner wakes from his bed of dust, the first thing he will see will be the Great White Throne and the Judge seated upon it. (See Revelation 20:11.) The first sound that will greet his ears will be the trumpet sounding this call:

> Come to judgment, come to judgment,
> Come to judgment, sinner, come.

He will look up to see the Son of Man on His judgment throne with the King's officers arranged on either side, the saints on His right hand and angels round about Him. Then the books will be opened (Revelation 20:12). What creeping horror will come upon the flesh of the wicked man! He knows his turn will arrive in a moment; he stands expecting it. Fear grips him while the eyes of the Judge look him through and through. He cries to the rocks to hide him and the mountains to fall upon him. (See Revelation 6:16.) Happy would he be now to find a friendly shelter in the grave, but the grave has burst its doors and can never be closed upon him again. He would even be glad to rush back to his former state in hell, but he must not. The Judgment has come; the indictment is set. Again the trumpet rings,

> Come to judgment, come to judgment,
> Come to judgment, come away.

Then the Book of Life is opened, and the dreadful sentence is pronounced. We discover this in the words of Scripture:

> [14] *And death and hell were cast into the lake of fire. This is the second death.*

¹⁵ *And whosoever was not found written in the book of life was cast into the lake of fire.* (Revelation 20:14–15)

The condemned sinner never knew what death was before. The first death was just a flea bite, but this is death indeed. The first death he might have looked back upon as a dream compared with this taste of death, now that the Lord has come.

As to Pain

From what we can glean darkly from hints in Scripture, the pains of death are not at all comparable to the pains of the Judgment at the Second Advent. Who could speak in a minimizing manner of the pains of death? If we should attempt to do so, we know that our hearts would contradict us.

In the shades of night, when deep sleep has enveloped you, you sometimes awake abruptly. You are alarmed. The terror by night has come upon you. You expect something— you hardly know what it coming—but you are half-afraid that you are about to die. You know how the cold sweat comes over you suddenly. You may have a good hope through grace, but the very thought of death brings a peculiar shudder.

Again, when death has really come into view, some of us, with terrible grief, have observed the sufferings of our dearest friends. We have heard the belabored gasping for breath. We have seen the face all pallid and the cheeks all hollow and sunken. We have sometimes seen how every nerve has become a road for the hot feet of pain to travel on, and how every vein has become a canal of grief. We have marked the pains, moans, groans, and dying strife that frighten the soul away. These, however, are common to man.

Not so are the pangs that are to be inflicted both on the body and on the soul at the Son of God's return. They are such that I want to veil them, fearful of the very thought. Let the Master's words suffice: *"Fear him, which after he hath killed hath power to cast into hell; yea, I say unto you, Fear him"* (Luke 12:5). Then the body in all its parts will suffer. The members that were once instruments of unrighteousness will now be instruments of suffering. The mind, which has sinned the most, will be the greatest sufferer. The memory, the judgment, the understanding, the will, the imagination, and every power and passion of the soul will become a deep lake of anguish.

I want to spare you these things. Do spare yourself! God knows with what anguish I even touch on these horrors. If they did not have to be addressed (and they must be, or else I must give my account at the Day of Judgment as a faithless servant), and if I did not have to express them now in mercy for your soul, poor sinner, I would just as soon forget them altogether, seeing that my own soul has a hope in Him who saves from the wrath to come.

But, as long as you will not have mercy upon yourself, I must lay this ax at your root. As long as you will make a mockery of sin and consider the terrors of the world to come as nothing, I must sternly warn you of hell. If it is hard to write about these things, what must it be to endure them? If a dream makes you quiver from head to foot, what must it be to endure, really and personally, the wrath to come?

Beloved, if I were to address you now as I should, my knees would be trembling and knocking together. If you were to feel as you should, there would not be an unconverted person reading this who would not cry, *"What must I do to be saved?"* (Acts 16:30). I urge you to remember that death, with all its pangs, is but a drop in a bucket compared with the deep, mysterious, fathomless, shoreless sea of grief that you must endure forever at the coming of the Lord Jesus, unless you repent.

In Regard to Discovery

Death makes great discoveries. The sinner thought himself to be wise, but death drew the curtain, and he saw written in large letters, "You fool!" He thought he was prudent as he hoarded up his gold and silver and kept back the wages of his laborers (see James 5:3–4), but he discovered that he had made a bad bargain when the question was put to him: "What did it profit you to have gained the whole world, but to have lost your soul?" (Mark 8:36).

Death is a great revealer of secrets. Many men are not believers at all until they die, but death comes and makes short work of their skepticism. Death deals one blow to the head of doubt, and it is all over. The man believes then, but his belief has come too late. Death gives to the sinner the discovery that there is a God, an angry God, and that punishment is wrapped up in the wrath to come.

Even so, how much greater are the discoveries that await the wayward one on the Day of Judgment! What will the sinner see then? He will see the Man who was crucified, sitting on the throne. He will hear how Satan has been defeated in all of his craftiest undertakings. When those mysterious books are read, the secrets of all hearts will be revealed. Men will understand how the Lord reigned supremely even when Satan roared most loudly. They will finally grasp how the mischief and folly of man brought forth the great purposes of God in the end. All of this will be in the books.

The sinner will stand there defeated, terribly defeated, ruined at every point, baffled, foiled, stultified in every act and every purpose by which he thought to do well for himself. Moreover, he will be utterly confounded in all the hostility and all the negligence of his heart toward the living and true God, who would and who did rule over him. Too late, he will realize the preciousness of the blood he despised, the value of the Savior he rejected, the glory of the heaven that he lost, the terror of the hell to which he is sentenced. How dreadfully wise he will be when fully aware of his terrible, eternal destruction! Thus, sinners will not discover what it truly means to taste of death until the Lord returns.

A Full Taste of Death

In the case of those who have physically died, they have not fully tasted of death, nor will they do so until Christ comes again. The moment a man dies, his spirit goes before God. If he is without Christ, his spirit then begins to feel the anger and the wrath of God. This is like a man being taken before a magistrate. He is known to be guilty, and so he is remanded to prison until his trial is scheduled. Such is the state of souls who are apart from their bodies. They are spirits in prison, awaiting trial.

There is not, in the sense in which the Catholics teach, any purgatory, from which there is a possibility of escape. Yet, there is a place of waiting for lost spirits that in Scripture is called "hell." It is one room in that awful prison in which spirits who die impenitent and without faith in Christ are doomed to dwell forever.

Bodily Suffering

Just consider why those of our departed countrymen who die without Christ have not yet fully tasted of death, and cannot do so until the Second Coming. First, their bodies do not suffer. The bodies of the wicked are still the prey of the worms, but they feel nothing. The atoms are still the sport of the winds, traversing their endless cycles until they will be gathered up again into their bodies at the sound of the last trumpet—at the voice of God.

The ungodly know that their present state is to have an end at the Last Judgment, but afterwards, their state will have no ending. It is then to go on and on, forever unchanged. There may be half a hope at present, an anticipation of some change, for change brings some relief. But, to the finally damned, upon whom the sentence has been pronounced, there is no hope even of a change. Forever and ever there will be the same ceaseless wheel of misery.

The Shame of Public Sentencing

The ungodly, too, in their present state, have not as yet been put to the shame of a public sentence. They have, as it were, merely been cast into prison, the facts being too clear to admit any doubt as to the sentence. They are their own tormentors, vexing and paining themselves with the fear of what is yet to come. They have never yet heard that dreadful sentence: *"Depart from me, ye cursed, into everlasting fire, prepared for the devil and his angels"* (Matthew 25:41).

While studying this subject, I was surprised to find how little is said about the pains of the lost while they are merely souls and how much is said concerning the pains they will have when the Lord returns. In the parable of the rich man and Lazarus, we see that the soul is already being tormented in the flames. (See

Luke 16:19–31.) But, if you read the parable of
the tares in the thirteenth chapter of Matthew,
we find it is at the end of the world that the
tares are to be cast into the fire.

The Eternal Lake of Fire

Following the parable of the tares comes
the parable of the dragnet in Matthew 13:47–
50. When the dispensation comes to an end,
the net is to be dragged to shore, and the good
are to be put in vessels while the bad are to be
cast away. The Lord said,

> [41] *The Son of man shall send forth his an-
> gels, and they shall gather out of his king-
> dom all things that offend, and them
> which do iniquity;*
> [42] *And shall cast them into a furnace of
> fire: there shall be wailing and gnashing
> of teeth.*   (Matthew 13:41–42)

We read in Matthew that memorable description of those of whom Christ will say, *"I
was an hungered, and ye gave me no meat: I
was thirsty, and ye gave me no drink"* (Matthew 25:42). This event is prophesied to occur
*"when the Son of man shall come in his glory,
and all the holy angels with him"* (v. 31).

In his second letter to the Thessalonians,
Paul, too, tells us plainly that the wicked are to

be destroyed at Christ's coming by the radiance of His power (2 Thessalonians 1:7–9). The recompense of the ungodly, like the reward of the righteous, is anticipated now, but the full reward of the righteous will be at His coming. They will reign with Christ. Their fullness of bliss will be given when the King Himself sits on His throne in all His glory. So, too, the wicked will have the beginning of their heritage at death, but the terrible fullness of it will be thereafter.

At the present moment, death and hell are not yet cast into the lake of fire. Death is still abroad in the world, slaying men. Hell is yet loose. The Devil is not yet chained. He still is going *"through dry places, seeking rest, and find*[ing] *none"* (Matthew 12:43). At the Last Day, at the Second Coming, *"death and hell* [will be] *cast into the lake of fire. This is the second death"* (Revelation 20:14). We do not completely understand the symbolism, but if it means anything, one would think it must mean that on that Day the scattered powers of evil, which are to be the tormentors of the wicked but which have hitherto been wandering throughout the world, will all be collected together. Then, indeed, it will be that the wicked begin to *"taste of death"* as they have never tasted of it before!

My soul is bowed down with terror while I write this. I scarcely know how to find suitable words to express the weight of thought that is upon me. Beloved, instead of speculating about these matters, let us try to shun the wrath to come. What can help us to do that better than to weigh the warning words of our loving Savior? He tells us that at His coming such a doom will pass upon impenitent souls that, compared with it, even death itself will be as nothing. Christians swallow death in victory (see 1 Corinthians 15:54) through their faith in the risen Lord; but if you die as an impenitent soul, you swallow death in ignorance. You do not feel its bitterness now. But, unless you repent, that bitter pill has yet to work its way, and that dire potion has yet to be drunk to the dregs.

Examine Your Heart

Does our study of these awful terrors prompt a question in you? Jesus said, *"Verily I say unto you, There be some standing here, which shall not taste of death, till they see the Son of man coming in his kingdom."* Are there any of you reading this who will taste of death when the Son of Man returns?

O beloved, try your own hearts, and since you may fail in the trial, ask the Lord to search you. As the Lord God lives, unless you search yourselves and find that you are on the right path, you may come to sit at the Lord's table presumptuously. (See Matthew 22:11–14.)

Deceitful Sinners

In that little group addressed by the Savior stood Judas. He had been trusted by his Master, and he was an apostle, but he was a thief and a hypocrite after all. He, *"the son of perdition"* (John 17:12), would not taste of death until Christ should come into His kingdom. Is there a Judas reading these words?

Many of you are members of Christian churches, but are you sure that you have made sound work of it? Is your belief genuine? Do you wear a mask, or are you honest? You may be self-proclaimed among His people here on the earth, but you may have to taste of death when the Lord comes. You may deceive them, but you cannot deceive Him.

Even if you are a preacher, you can reflect that you may be mistaken, that you may be self-deceived. If it is so, may the Lord open your eyes to know the truth of your own state.

Will you offer a prayer of repentance for yourselves, you who profess to know Christ? Do not be too bold or too quick, you who say you are Christ's. Never be satisfied until you are absolutely sure. The best way to be sure is to go again, just as you went at first, and seize eternal life through the power of the blessed Spirit and not by any strength of your own.

Careless Sinners

No doubt, however, there stood in that throng around the Savior some who were careless sinners. He knew that there had been some during His entire ministry and that there would still be some. Thus, they would taste of death at His coming. Are there not some careless, unconcerned people reading this right now? You who rarely think about religion, you who generally view Sunday as a day of pleasure or who lounge around in your sports clothes the whole day, you who look upon the very name of religion as a monster to frighten children with, you who mock God's servants and condemn the very thought of earnestly seeking after the Most High—will you be among the number of those who taste of death when the Son of Man comes in His kingdom? Must I ring your death knell now? Must my warning be lost upon you? I urge you to recollect that you must either turn or burn. I entreat you to remember this:

> ⁷ *Let the wicked forsake his way, and the unrighteous man his thoughts: and let him return unto the LORD, and he will have mercy upon him; and to our God, for he will abundantly pardon.* (Isaiah 55:7)

By the wounds of Jesus, sinner, stop and think! Since God's dear Son was slain for human sin, how terrible must that sin be? Since Jesus died for you, how base are you if you are disobedient to the doctrine of faith? I implore you that, if you think of your body, give some thought to your soul.

> ² *Wherefore do ye spend money for that which is not bread? and your labour for that which satisfieth not? hearken diligently unto me, and eat ye that which is good, and let your soul delight itself in fatness.* (Isaiah 55:2)

Carefully focus on God's Word, and eat of that which is good, real, substantial food. Come to Jesus, so that you may live eternally.

Willful Sinners

Around Jesus were some of another class: the willfully unrepentant Bethsaida and Capernaum sinners. (See Matthew 11:21–24.) Likewise, there are some of you who constantly occupy church pews and sit in services Sunday after Sunday. The same eyes look at the pastor week after week. The same faces salute him often with a smile when Sunday comes. Yet, how many of you are still without God and without Christ?

Have we preachers been unfaithful to you? If we have, forgive us, and pray, both for us and for yourselves, that we all may mend our ways. But, if we have warned you of the wrath to come, why do you choose to walk in the path that leads to it? If we have preached Christ Jesus to you, how is it that His charms do not move you and that the story of His great love does not bring you to repentance? May the Spirit of God deal with you, for man cannot. Our hammers do not break your flinty hearts, but God's arm can do it. May He turn you yet.

Of all sinners over whom a minister ought to weep, you are the worst, for while the careless perish, you perish doubly. You know your Master's will, and yet you do not do it. You see heaven's gate set open, and yet you will not enter. Your vicious free will ruins you. Your base, wicked love of self and sin destroys you. Jesus said, *"And ye will not come to me, that ye might have life"* (John 5:40). You are so stubborn that you will not turn even though Jesus woos you. I do pray that you will let the terror of the Judgment presented here stir you now as you have never been stirred before. May God have pity on you even if you will have no pity on yourselves.

Prostituting Sinners

Among that company perhaps there were some who held to the truth, but who were behaving immorally. Some of you who are reading this may be like those people. You believe in eternal election, as I do, but you make it a cloak for your sin. You hold to the doctrine of the perseverance of the saints, but you still continue in your iniquity. Perhaps there is no worse way of perishing than perishing by making the doctrines of grace an excuse for one's sins. The apostle Paul has well said of such that their *"damnation is just"* (Romans 3:8). God's condemnation of any man is just, but to a sevenfold degree is it just for such a person.

I would not have you forget this doctrine, nor neglect it, nor despise it. But, I beg you, do not prostitute it. Do not turn it to the vile purpose of making it pander to your own carnal desires. Remember, you have no evidence of election except that you are holy, and you have no right to expect you will be saved at the last unless you are saved now. A present faith in a present Savior is the key.

Redeemed Sinners

May my Master bring some of you to trust Him right now. The plan of salvation is simple. Trust Christ, and you are saved. Rely upon Him, and you will live. This faith is the gift of God, but remember that although God gives it, He *"worketh in you both to will and to do of his good pleasure"* (Philippians 2:13).

God does not believe for you; the Holy Spirit does not believe for you; you must believe, or else you will be lost. To say that it is also the act of man is quite consistent with the fact that it is the gift of God. You must, poor soul, be led to trust the Savior, or you can never enter into heaven. Are you saying, "I want to find the Savior now"? Do not go to bed until you have sought Him. Seek Him with sighs and with tears until you find Him.

I think now is a time of grace. I have painted a picture of the law and the terrors of the Lord for you, but now will be a time of grace to the souls of some of you. My Master kills you so that He may make you alive. (See 1 Samuel 2:6.) He wounds you only so that He may make you whole. (See Jeremiah 30:14–17.)

I feel an inward whisper in my heart that there are some of you who even now have begun your flight from the wrath to come. Where should you flee? Run to Jesus. Hurry, sinner, hurry. I trust you will find Him before you retire to your bed. Or, if you lie there, tossing about in doubt and fear, then may He manifest Himself to you before the morning light.

I would freely give my eyes so that you might see Christ, and I would willingly give my hands so that you might lay hold of Him. I implore you, do not put this warning away from you, but let it have its proper work in you and lead you to repentance. May God save you, and may the prayer of my heart be answered, that all of you be found among His elect at His right hand on that great and terrible Day.

Our Father,
Save us with Your great salvation. We pray, do not condemn us, Lord. Deliver us from going down to the pit, for You have found the ransom. May we not be among the company that shall taste of death when the Son of Man comes. Hear us, Jesus, through Your blood. God be merciful to us sinners.   Amen

Chapter Two

The Great White Throne

And I saw a great white throne,
and him that sat on it, from whose face
the earth and the heaven fled away;
and there was found no place for them.
—Revelation 20:11

Many of the visions that the apostle John saw are very obscure. Although a man who is assured of his own salvation may possibly be justified in spending his days endeavoring to interpret them, I am sure that it will not be a profitable task for unconverted people. They have no time to spare on speculations, for they have not yet secured for themselves the absolute certainties. They need not dive into difficulties, for they have not yet laid a foundation of the basic doctrines of faith in Christ Jesus. It is far better to meditate on the Atonement than to be guessing at the meaning of *"a little horn"* (Daniel 8:9). It is far better to know the Lord Jesus in His power to save than to devise an ingenious theory about *"the number of the beast"* (Revelation 13:18).

However, the particular vision in our text is so instructive, so unattended by serious difficulties, that I invite you to consider it. Even more, I do so because it has to do with matters that concern our own eternal prospects. It may be, if the Holy Spirit illuminates the eyes of our faith to look and see the *"great white throne and him that sat upon it,"* that we may reap so much benefit from the sight as to make all of heaven ring with gratitude that we were brought into this world to see the Great White Throne. By seeing it with the eyes of faith, we will not be afraid to look upon it in the Day when the Judge sits and the quick and dead stand before Him. (See Acts 10:42.)

First, I will endeavor to explain what John saw. Secondly, I will set forth the effect that I think would be produced by this sight if the eyes of our faith were now focused there.

John's Vision

First, then, I want to call your very earnest attention to what John saw. It was a scene of the Last Day—that wondrous Day whose coming none can foretell.

> For, as a thief unheard, unseen,
> It steals through night's dark shade.

A Throne of Moral Government

When the eagle-eyed prophet of Patmos, being in the Spirit, looked aloft into the heavens, he saw a throne. From this, I gather that there is a throne of moral government over the sons of men, and that He who sits upon it presides over all the inhabitants of this world. The dominion of this throne reaches from Adam in Paradise down to the last man on earth, whoever he may be. We are not without our Judge, Lawgiver, and King (Isaiah 33:22). This world is not left so that men may do in it as they will, without a governor, without an avenger, without anyone to give reward or to inflict punishment.

In his blindness, the sinner looks, but he sees no throne. Therefore, he cries, "I will live as I desire, for there is none to call me to account." However, John, with illumined eyes, distinctly saw a throne and a personal Ruler, who sat there to call His subjects to account. When our faith looks through the glass of revelation, it sees a throne, too.

It would be good for us if we felt more fully the influence of that ever present throne. Beloved, the fact that *"the LORD reigneth"* (Psalm 93:1) is true now and true at all times. There is a throne on which *"the King eternal, immortal, invisible"* (1 Timothy 1:17) sits. The world is governed by laws made and kept in force by the omniscient Lawgiver. There is one truly moral, righteous Judge. Men are responsible beings and will be brought to account for their actions at the Last Day, when they will all be either rewarded or punished.

"I saw a great white throne." How this invests the actions of men with solemnity! Even if we were left to do exactly as we wanted to without being called to account, it would still be wise to be virtuous. Rest assured, it is best for us to be good. To be evil is enough of a malady in and of itself.

However, we are not left to our own devices. There is a law laid down, the breaking of which involves a penalty. There is a Lawgiver who looks down and sees every action of man and who does not allow one single word or deed to be omitted from His notebook. That Judge is armed with power. He is coming soon to hold His great tribunal, and every responsible agent on the face of the earth must appear at His bar and receive sentencing, as we have been told:

> [10] *For we must all appear before the judgment seat of Christ; that every one may receive the things done in his body, according to that he hath done, whether it be good or bad.*   (2 Corinthians 5:10)

Let it, then, be understood from our text that there is indeed a personal and real moral Governor of the world, an efficient and suitable Ruler, not a mere name, not a myth, not an empty office, but a Person who sits on the throne, who judges righteously, and who will carry out that Judgment before long.

The Right to Rule

Now, brothers and sisters, we know that this moral Governor is God Himself, who has an undisputed right to reign and rule. Some thrones have no right to be, and to revolt from them is patriotism. However, the person who best loves his own race delights the most in the monarchy of heaven.

Doubtless, there are dynasties that are tyrannies and governors who are despots, but none may dispute the right of God to sit upon the Great White Throne or wish that another hand held the *"sceptre of righteousness"* (Hebrews 1:8). He created all; should He not judge all? As Creator, He had a right to set down His laws over His creation. Because those laws are the pattern of everything that is good and true, He had, therefore, an eternal right to govern, in addition to the right that belonged to Him as Creator. He is the Judge of all; He must do right from a necessity of His nature. Who else, then, should sit upon the throne, and who would dare to claim to do so? He may cast down the gauntlet to all His creatures and say, *"I am God, and there is none else"* (Isaiah 45:22). If He reveals the thunder of His power, His creatures must silently admit that He alone is Lord. None can venture to say that this throne is not founded upon right.

Moreover, there are some thrones on which the kings, however right, are deficient in might, but this is not the case with the King of Kings. We often see little princes whose crowns so poorly fit their heads that they cannot keep them on their brows. However, our God has invincible might as well as infallible right.

Who would meet Him in the battle? Will the stubble defy the fire, or will the wax make war with the flame? Jehovah can easily swallow up His enemies when they set themselves in battle array against Him. *"He looketh on the earth, and it trembleth: he toucheth the hills, and they smoke"* (Psalm 104:32). He breaks Leviathan in pieces in the depths of the sea

(Psalm 74:13–14). The clouds are His chariots, and He walks on the wings of the wind (Psalm 104:3). At His bidding there is day, and at His will night covers the earth (Genesis 1:3–5). *"Who can hinder him? who will say unto him, What doest thou?"* (Job 9:12). His throne is founded in right and supported by might. Justice and truth have settled it, and omnipotence and wisdom are its guards, so that it cannot be moved.

The Power of His Throne

Additionally, none can escape the power of His throne. At this moment, the sapphire throne of God (see Ezekiel 1:26) is revealed in heaven, where adoring men cast their crowns before it (Revelation 4:10). Its power is felt on earth, where the works of creation praise the Lord. Even those who do not acknowledge the divine government are compelled to feel it, for He does as He wills, not only among those in heaven, but also among the inhabitants of this lower world. Hell feels the terror of that throne. Those chains of fire, those pangs unutterable, are the awful shadow of the throne of Deity. As God looks upon the lost, the torment that flashes through their souls comes from His holiness, which cannot endure their sins.

The influence of that throne, then, is found in every world where spirits dwell. It also rules the realms of inanimate nature. Every leaf that fades in the trackless forest trembles at the Almighty's bidding. Every coral insect that dwells in the unfathomable depths of the sea feels and acknowledges the presence of the all-present King.

No Escape

So then, beloved, if such were the throne that John saw, see how impossible it will be for you to escape from the great tribunal when the Judgment Day is proclaimed and the Judge issues His summons bidding you to appear. Where can the enemies of God flee? If their high-flown impudence could carry them up to heaven, His right hand of holiness would hurl them there. If they could dive under hell's deepest wave, His left hand would pluck them out of the fire to expose them to the fiercer light of His countenance. Nowhere is there a refuge from the Most High. The morning beams cannot convey the fugitive so swiftly that the almighty Pursuer could not follow him. Neither can the mysterious lightning bolt, which annihilates time and space, journey so rapidly as to escape His far-reaching hand. *"If I ascend up into heaven, thou art there: if I make my bed in hell, behold, thou art there"* (Psalm 139:8).

It was said of the Roman Empire under the Caesars that the whole world was only one great big prison, because if any man offended the emperor, it was impossible to escape Caesar's reach. If the man crossed the Alps, could not Caesar find him in Gaul? If he sought to hide himself in the Indies, even there the swarthy monarchs knew the power of the Roman army, so that they would give no shelter to a man who had incurred imperial vengeance. And yet, perhaps, a fugitive from Rome might have prolonged his miserable life by hiding in the dens and caves of the earth.

But, sinner, there is no hiding from God. The mountains cannot cover you from Him, nor can the rocks conceal you. See, then, how this throne strikes our minds with awesome terror at the very outset. Founded in right, sustained by might, and universal in its dominion, look and see the throne beheld by the Beloved Apostle.

Purity of the Throne

This, however, is but the beginning of the vision. Our text tells us that it was a *"white throne,"* and I call your attention to that. *"I saw a great white throne.*" Why white? Does this not indicate its immaculate purity? I fear there is no other white throne to be found. The throne of our own country I believe to be as white and as pure as any throne might well be on earth,[1] but there have been years, even in the annals of that throne, when it was stained with blood. Not always was it a throne of excellence and purity. Even now, although our throne possesses a lustrous purity—rare enough among earthly thrones—yet in the sight of God there must be something that is impure in everything that is earthly, and therefore the throne is not white to Him. As for many other thrones that are still in existence, we know all of them are not white.

This is neither the day nor the hour for us to call earthly princes to the bar of God, but some of them will have much to answer for, because, in their self-aggrandizing schemes, they took no account of the blood that would be shed or of the rights that would be violated. Principle seldom moves the royal mind, but the roguish law of policy is the basis of a king's decision—a policy worthy of highwaymen and burglars—and some kings are small-minded.

---

[1] This is a reference to Alexandrina Victoria, queen of Great Britain from 1837 to 1901, Her reign was a model of purity and virtue to the world.

On the continent of Europe, there are more than a few thrones that I might describe as either black or crimson, as I think of the depravity of the conduct of the monarch or of the blood through which he has waded his way to dominion.

However, this is *"a great white throne,"* a throne of holy monarchy that is not stained with blood or defiled with injustice. Why, then, is it white for purity? Is it not because the King who sits on it is pure? Listen to the sacred hymn of the cherubic band and the seraphic choir: *"Holy, holy, holy, is the LORD of hosts"* (Isaiah 6:3). Creatures who are perfectly spotless themselves will unceasingly adore and reverence the superior holiness of the great King. He is too great to need to be unjust, and He is too good to be unkind. This King has done no wrong and can do no wrong, but He is the only king of whom this can be said without fiction. He who sits on this white throne is the essence of holiness, justice, truth, and love. O fairest of all thrones! Who would not be a willing subject of your peerless government?

Moreover, the throne is pure because the law the Judge dispenses is perfect! There is no fault in the Statute Book of God. When the Lord comes to judge the earth, there will be found no decree that bears too harshly upon

51

any one of His creatures. *"The statutes of the LORD are right...the judgments of the LORD are true and righteous altogether"* (Psalm 19:8–9). Who can improve the Book that contains the Ten Commandments, in which you find a summary of the divine will? Who can find anything in excess in it or point out anything that is lacking? *"The law of the LORD is perfect, converting the soul"* (Psalm 19:7), and well may the throne be white from which there emanates such a law.

However, you know that, even with a good law and a good lawgiver, sometimes the throne may make mistakes, and it may be stained by ignorance, if not by willful injustice. Yet, the sentence that will go forth from this Great White Throne will be so consistent with justice that even the condemned culprit himself must give his unwilling assent to it. Christ said of the guilty guest, *"He was speechless"* (Matthew 22:12)—speechless because he could neither bear the sentence nor in any way contradict it.

It is a white throne, since never was a verdict delivered from it of which the culprit had a right to complain. Perhaps there are some who view this as a matter of hope, but to ungodly people it will be the very reverse. Sinner, if you had to be judged before an impure tribunal, you might escape. If the judge were not holy, unholiness might go unpunished. If the law were not perfect, offenses might be condoned. Or, if the sentence were not just, you might escape through partiality. However, where everything is so pure and white,

Careless sinner,
What will there become of you?

A Noticeable Throne

I have also thought that perhaps this throne is said to be a white throne to indicate that it will be eminently conspicuous. You may have noticed that a white object can be seen from a very great distance. Perhaps you have observed a white cottage far away on the mountains, standing out noticeably. Often, the residents like to make their cottages intensely white so that, though you would not have perceived it had it been left a stone color, you see it at once, because the bright, whitewashed walls catch your eye. I suppose marksmen prefer white to almost any other color for their targets.

Likewise, this Great White Throne will be so conspicuous that the millions who were dead, but who rise at the last trumpet, will all see it. It will not be possible for a single eye to close itself against the sight. We must see it. It will be so striking a sight that none of us will be able to prevent its coming before us: *"every eye shall see"* (Revelation 1:7).

Possibly it is called a white throne because it is such a convincing contrast to all the colors of this sinful human life. There stand the crowds, and here is the Great White Throne. What can make them see their blackness more thoroughly than to stand there in contrast with the perfection of the law and the Judge? Perhaps that throne, all glistening, will reflect each man's character. As each unforgiven man looks at that throne, its dazzling whiteness will overcome him, covering him with confusion and terror when he sees his own defilement in contrast with it. He will cry, "O God, how can I bear to be judged by You? I could face the judgment seat of my peers, for I could see imperfections in my judges, but I cannot face You, dreadful Supreme, for the pure whiteness of Your throne and the terrible splendor of Your holiness utterly overwhelm me. Who am I, sinner as I am, that I should dare to stand before that Great White Throne?"

The Greatness of the Throne

The other adjective that John used in describing the throne is *"great."* It is a *"great*

white throne." You scarcely need me to tell you
that it is called a Great White Throne because
of the greatness of Him who sits upon it. Have
you heard of the greatness of Solomon? He was
but a petty prince. Do you speak of the thrones
of Rome and Greece, before which multitudes
of beings assembled, or of the throne of the
Mogul, His Celestial Majesty of China? They
are as nothing, mere representatives of asso-
ciations of the grasshoppers of the world, in
the sight of God Almighty.

A throne filled by a mortal is but a shadow
of dominion. However, this will be a great
throne because on it will sit the great God of
the earth, heaven, and hell; *"the King eternal,
immortal, invisible"* (1 Timothy 1:17), who will
judge the world with righteousness and His
people with equity (Psalm 98:9).

Multitudes before the Throne

Beloved, you can see that this will be a
"great white throne" when you remember the
culprits who will be brought before it—not a
handful of criminals, but millions upon millions, *"multitudes, multitudes in the valley of
decision"* (Joel 3:14). These will not all be of
the lesser sort, not just serfs and slaves whose
miserable bodies rested from their oppressors

in silent graves, but the great ones of the earth will be there. The downtrodden serf who toiled for nothing and felt it sweet to die will not be alone, but his tyrant master who grew fat on his unrewarded toils will be there. The multitudes who marched to battle at their master's bidding and who fell beneath shots and shells will not be alone, but the emperors and kings who planned the conflict will be there, crowned heads no greater than the uncrowned. Men who were demigods among their contemporaries will be mingled with their slaves and will be as vile as they.

What a marvelous procession! With what awe the imagination of it strikes the heart! You who were downtrodden, the great Leveler has put you all upon the same footing now. Death laid you in one equal grave, and now Judgment finds you standing at one equal tribunal, to receive the sentence of One who fears no king and dreads no tyrant, who is *"no respecter of persons"* (Acts 10:34), but who metes out justice the same way to all.

Can you picture the sight? Land and sea are covered with the living who once were dead. Hell is empty, and the grave has lost its victims. What a sight that will be! Xerxes, the great king of Persia, with a million parading before him, must have seen a grand spectacle, but what will this be? No flaunting banner, but the colors of eternal majesty. No gaudy courtiers, but assembled angels. No drum beat or cannon roar, but the blast of the archangel's trumpet and the harps of ten thousand times ten thousand holy ones. There will be unrivaled splendor, but not that of heraldry and war. Mere tinsel and baubles will have all vanished. In their place will be the splendor of flashing lightning and the deep bass of thunder. Then, Jesus, the Man of Sorrows, with all His angels, will descend, the pomp of heaven being revealed to the sons of men.

Eternal Judgments from the Throne

It is a Great White Throne because of the matters that will be tried there. These will not be petty quarrels over a suit in litigation or an estate in jeopardy. Our souls will be tried there—our future, not for an age, not for one single century, but forever. Upon those balances will hang heaven and hell. To the right will be distributed triumph without end; to the left, destruction and confusion without pause; and the destiny of every person will be positively declared from that tremendous throne. Can you perceive its greatness? You must comprehend heaven; you must fathom hell; you must measure eternity. Until you do, you will not know the greatness of this Great White Throne.

Remembering the Judgments from the Throne

The throne is great because the transactions of that Day will repeatedly be recalled throughout eternity. Judgment Day will be unto you, you saints, a *"beginning of days"* (Hebrews 7:3), when Christ says to you, *"Come, ye blessed of my Father"* (Matthew 25:34).

That Day will be to you who perish a beginning, too, just as that famous Passover night in Egypt was. When the firstborn were spared in every house where a lamb had shed its blood, it was the first of days to Israel; but to Egypt, the night when the firstborn felt the avenging angel's sword was a dreadful beginning of nights forever. Many a mother counted time from that night when the destroyer came, and throughout eternity, you will likewise calculate from the day when you see the Great White Throne.

The Righteous Judge on the Throne

Do not avert your eyes from the magnificent spectacle until you have seen the glorious

Person mentioned in the words, *"and him that sat on it."* I wonder whether anything I have written has made you solemnly ponder the events of that Last Day. I fear I cannot write so as to get at your hearts. But, for a moment, think about Him who sits upon the Great White Throne.

The most fitting One in all the world sits upon that throne. He is God; but, remember, He is also man. *"He will judge the world in righteousness by that man"* (Acts 17:31), wrote Doctor Luke; *"God shall judge...by Jesus Christ according to my gospel"* (Romans 2:16), said the apostle Paul. The Judge must be God. Who but God is fit to judge so many and so exactly? The throne is too great for any but Him of whom it is written, *"Thy throne, O God, is for ever and ever: a sceptre of righteousness is the sceptre of thy kingdom"* (Hebrews 1:8).

Christ Jesus, the Son of God, will judge. He will judge as man as well as God. How fitting it is that it should be so! As man, He knows our infirmities (Hebrews 4:15) and understands our hearts and minds (1 Chronicles 28:9), so we cannot object to Him. Our Judge Himself should be like we are. Who could better judge with righteous justice than the One who is *"bone of* [our] *bones, and flesh of* [our] *flesh"* (Genesis 2:23)?

And then, there is this rightness about it. He is not only God and man, but He is the Man, the Man of men, of all men the most manly, the type and pattern of manhood. He will be the model in His own person, for if a man is like Christ, that man is righteous, but if a man is other than Christlike, that man deserves to be condemned. That wondrous Judge needs only to look upon His own character to read the law; He needs only to review His own actions to discern whether other men's actions are right or wrong. The thoughts of many hearts were revealed by Christ when He was on earth, and that same Christ will make an open exhibition of men at the great Judgment. He will judge them. He will discern their spirits. He will find out the joints and the marrow of their beings—He will lay bare *"the thoughts and intents of the heart"* (Hebrews 4:12).

Believer, you will pass before His throne, too. Let no man deceive you with the delusion that you will not be judged. The sheep, as well as the goats, appeared before the Good Shepherd who separated them (see Matthew 25:32–33); those who used their talents were called to account as well as he who buried his (see Matthew 25:14–30); and the disciples themselves were warned that they would account for every idle word at the Judgment (Matthew 12:36).

You do not need to fear a public trial. Innocence courts the light. You will not be saved by being smuggled into heaven untested and unproved, but you will pass the solemn test with joy in the righteousness of Jesus. The righteous may not be judged at the same time as the wicked (I am not contending about particulars), but I am certain that the righteous will be judged and that Christ's blood has been provided for this very reason, so that they may find the mercy of the Lord in that Day.

O sinner, it is far otherwise for you, for your ruin is sure when the time of testing comes. There will be no witnesses needed to convict you, for the Judge knows all. Jesus Christ, whom you despised, will judge you. The Savior, whose mercy you trampled on, in the fountain of whose blood you would not wash, who was *"despised and rejected of men"* (Isaiah 53:3)—it is He who will bring righteous justice to you. What will He be able to say but this: *"But those mine enemies, which would not that I should reign over them, bring hither, and slay them before me"* (Luke 19:27)?

Practical Application of the Vision

At this point, I want to draw the inferences that flow from such a sight as the Great

White Throne and thus give John's vision practical relevance.

A Believer's Examination of Self

Believer in Christ, I have a question for you: Can you see the Great White Throne and He who sits upon it? May your response be like this: "I think I see it now. Let me search myself. Whatever profession I may make, I will have to face that Great White Throne. I have been approved by the pastor and the elders. I stand accepted by the church. Still, that Great White Throne is not passed yet. I have borne a reputable character among my fellow Christians. I have prayed in public, and my prayers have been much admired. But, I have not yet been weighed in the last balances. What if I should be found wanting?" (See Daniel 5:27.)

Beloved Christian, what about your private prayers? Can you neglect your prayer closet and yet remember that your prayers will be tried before the Great White Throne? Is your Bible left unread in private? Is your religion nothing but a public show and sham? Remember the Great White Throne, because pretense will not pass there.

Fellow believer, what about your heart and your treasure? Are you merely seeking after material possessions? Do you live as others who are not believers live? Is your delight in the fleeting present? Do you have dealings with the throne of heaven? Have you a stony heart toward divine things? Have you little love for Christ? Do you make an empty profession of faith and nothing more? Oh, think of that Great White Throne!

Some people, when I preach a stirring sermon, feel afraid to come again to hear me. Do searching sermons seem to go through you like a blast of the north wind, chilling you to the marrow and curdling your blood? Friend, if you are afraid of the pastor's voice, how will you bear His voice who will speak in tones of thunder? Oh, what must it be to stand before that dreadful tribunal? Are you doubting now? What will you be then? Can you not bear a little self-examination now? If not, how will you bear that God-examination? If earthly scales tell you that you are wanting, what message will the scales of heaven give you?

I am writing to you as I would address my own heart, and I entreat you, professing Christians, *"Examine yourselves, whether ye be in the faith; prove your own selves. Know ye not your own selves, how that Jesus Christ is in you, except you be reprobates?"* (2 Corinthians 13:5).

Hypocrites

Having directed a word to the Christian, I now write to all of you, in recalling this Great White Throne, to shun hypocrisy. Are you tempted to be baptized, although you are not a believer, in order to please your parents and friends? Beware of that Great White Throne, and think how your insult to God will look at that Last Day! Are you persuaded to put on the cloak of religion and carry on your deceitful masquerade simply because it will help your business or make you seem respectable? Beware, you hypocrite, beware of that Great White Throne.

Of all the terrors that will come forth from it, there will be none more severe than those that will scathe the mere pretender who made a profession of religion for personal gain. If you must be damned, be damned in any way other than as a hypocrite, for they deserve the deepest hell who, for the sake of gain, make a profession of godliness. The ruin of expediency and hypocrisy will be just indeed. O you high-flying professors, whose wings (like those of the mythological Icarus) are fastened on with wax, beware of the sun that will surely pour its heat on you. Fearful will be your fall from so great a height!

Unrepentant Sinners

But there are some of you who say, "I do not make any profession of faith." Nevertheless, our text has a word for you, and I want you to judge your actions by that Last Great Day. O reader, how about that night of sin? "No," you say, "never mind it; do not bring it to my remembrance." But, it will be brought to your remembrance, and that deed of sin will be proclaimed far wider than just from the housetops. It will be spread to all the multitudes who have ever lived since the first man, and your infamy will become *"a proverb and a byword among all people"* (1 Kings 9:7). What do you think of this, you secret sinners, you lovers of wantonness and debauchery?

Ah, young man, you have commenced by filching, but you will go on to be a downright thief. It is not hidden to all, so *"be sure your sin will find you out"* (Numbers 32:23). Young woman, you have begun to dally with sin. You think no one has seen you, but the Mighty One has seen your acts and heard your words. There is no curtain between Him and your sin. He sees you clearly, and what will you do with these sins of yours that you think have been concealed? "It was many years ago," you tell me. Yes, but, although buried to you, they are all alive to Him, for everything is present to the all-seeing God. Your forgotten deeds will one day stand out very presently to you, also.

Dear readers, I entreat you to do nothing that you would not do if you thought God was watching you, for He does see you. Look at your actions in the light of the Judgment. That secret drinking of yours, how will that look when God reveals it? That private lust of yours that nobody knows about, how would you dare even think about it if you recollected that God knows it? Young man, it is a secret, a fearful secret, and you would not whisper it in anyone's ear. But, it will be whispered—no, it will be thundered out before the world. I pray that you would think of this. There is an Observer who takes note of all that we do and will publish all to an assembled universe.

As for us all, are we ready to meet that Last Great Day? If tonight the trumpet should be sounded, what would be your state of mind? Suppose that right now every ear should be startled with a loud and dreadful blast, and a voice were heard as it called,

Come to judgment, come to judgment,
Come to judgment, come away.

Suppose that some of you could hide in the closets and in the basements, would not many rush to find concealment? How few of us might go walking steadily into the open air and saying, "I am not afraid of the Judgment, for *'there is therefore now no condemnation to them which are in Christ Jesus'*" (Romans 8:1)!

Facing Judgment with Assurance

Brothers and sisters, I hope there are some of us who would go gladly to that judgment seat, even if we had to traverse the jaws of death to reach it. I hope there are some of us who can sing this in our hearts:

> Bold shall I stand in that great day;
> For who aught to my charge shall lay?
> While, through thy blood, absolved I am
> From sin's tremendous curse and blame.

Many of us might be very much put out to say that. It is easy to speak of full assurance, but, believe me, it is not quite so easy to have it in absolute earnest in trying times. If some of you get a finger ache, your confidence oozes out at your joints, and if you have but a little sickness, you think, "Oh, it may be cancer; what will I do?" If you cannot bear to die, how then will you bear to live forever? If you cannot look death in the face without a shudder, then how will you endure the Judgment?

Could you gaze upon death and feel that it is your friend and not your foe? Could you keep a skull on your nightstand and contemplate it as your reminder of death? It may well take the bravest of us to face death so fearlessly. The only sure way to do so is to come as we are to Jesus, with no righteousness of our own to trust in, but finding all we need in Him. (See Philippians 3:9.)

When William Carey[2] was about to die, he ordered this verse to be put on his tombstone:

> A guilty, weak, and helpless worm,
> On Christ's kind arms I fall,
> He is my strength, my righteousness,
> My Jesus, and my all.

I would like to wake up in eternity with such a verse as that in my mind. Likewise, I wish to go to sleep in this world with such a hope as this in my heart:

> Nothing in my hand I bring,
> Simply to the cross I cling.

Time Can Catch You Off Guard

I am referring to themes that you may think are far removed, but just changing your

---

[2] William Carey (1761–1834), missionary to India, called the "father of modern missions."

perspective can bring them near to you. A thousand years is a long time, but how soon it flies! While reading English history, we almost seem to go back and shake hands with William the Conqueror. Going further back in time a few more generations quickly brings us to the Flood. As we look backward, millenia seem to be nothing.

You who are approaching the age of fifty, and especially you who are sixty or seventy, must feel how fast time flies. I seem to preach a sermon one Sunday only in time to get ready for the next. Time rushes by with such a whirl that no express train can overtake it, and even a flash of lightning seems to lag behind it.

We will soon be at the Great White Throne. We will soon be at the judgment bar of God. Let us be making ready for it. Let us not live so much in this present time, which is but a dream or an empty shadow, but let us live in the real, substantial future.

Oh, may I reach some heart right now! I have a notion that there is someone reading this who will not have another warning. Who among my readers will it be who will die this week, beyond hope? Ponder the question well! Will you be the one to dwell in the devouring flames if you do not repent right now? Will you abide in everlasting fire? If I knew you, I would willingly cover you with tears. If I knew you who are to die this week, I would find you, kneel down at your side, and urge you to think of eternal things. But I do not know you, and therefore, by the living God, I implore you all to fly to Jesus by faith.

Be Prepared

These are no trifling matters, are they? If they are, I am but a sorry trifler, and you may laugh at me. But, if they are true and real, it suits me to be in earnest, and how much more it will suit you to be so. Prepare to meet your God. He is coming, so prepare now for that Day! *"Behold, now is the accepted time; behold, now is the day of salvation"* (2 Corinthians 6:2). The gates of mercy are not closed. Your sin is not unpardonable. You may yet find mercy. Christ invites you. His blood-drops cry to you:

Come and welcome,
Come and welcome, sinner, come.

May the Holy Spirit put life into these simple words of mine, and may the Lord help you to come to Him now. The way to come is just to trust in Christ. It is all done when you trust in Christ. Throw yourselves on Him and His mercy, putting your trust in nothing else.

Just now I am resting my entire weight in a sturdy old chair, but should this chair give way, I would fall. Lean on Christ in that same way. Risk everything with Christ; trust nothing else but Him. If you can get a grip on the Cross and stand there beneath the crimson canopy of the atoning blood, God Himself cannot smite you, and the Judgment Day will dawn upon you with splendor and delight, instead of gloom and terror.

Return, O wanderer, to thy home,
Thy Father calls for thee;
No longer now an exile roam
In guilt and misery.
Return, return.

Return, O wanderer, to thy home,
'Tis Jesus calls for thee:
"The Spirit and the bride say, Come,"[3]
Oh, now for refuge flee.
Return, return.

Return, O wanderer, to thy home,
'Tis madness to delay
There are no pardons in the tomb,
And brief is mercy's day.
Return, return.

---

[3] Revelation 22:17

Chapter Three

The Watchword for Today

For our conversation is in heaven; from whence also we look for the Saviour, the Lord Jesus Christ: who shall change our vile body, that it may be fashioned like unto his glorious body, according to the working whereby he is able even to subdue all things unto himself. Therefore, my brethren, dearly beloved and longed for, my joy and crown, so stand fast in the Lord, my dearly beloved.
—Philippians 3:20—4:1

*E*very doctrine of the Word of God has its practical application. As each tree bears seed after its kind, so does every truth of God bring forth practical virtues. Hence, you find the apostle Paul very full of *therefores*—his *therefores* being the conclusions drawn from certain statements of divine truth. I marvel that the early translators who codified the Holy Scriptures divided the argument from the conclusion by making a new chapter where there is least reason for it.

I want to remind you of the surest and most certain resurrection of our Lord Jesus. There is a practical force in that truth, which constitutes part of what is meant by *"the power of his resurrection"* (Philippians 3:10). Since the Lord has risen, He will surely come a second time, when He will raise the bodies of His people at His return.

That is something to wait for and a grand reason for steadfastness while we are waiting. We are looking for the coming of our Lord and Savior, Jesus Christ, from heaven and anticipating that He will *"change our vile body, that it may be fashioned like unto his glorious body."* Therefore, let us stand fast in the position that will secure us this honor. Let us keep our posts until the coming of the great Captain releases us from our sentinel watch.

Our glorious resurrection will abundantly repay us for all the toil and travail we have to undergo for the Lord in the battle. *"For I reckon that the sufferings of this present time are not worthy to be compared with the glory which shall be revealed in us"* (Romans 8:18).

The glory to be revealed even now casts a light upon our path and causes sunshine within our hearts. The hope of this happiness makes us even now *"strong in the Lord, and in the power of his might"* (Ephesians 6:10).

Paul was deeply anxious that those in whom he had been the means of kindling the heavenly hope might be preserved faithful until the coming of Christ. He trembled for fear that any of them should seem to draw back and prove traitors to their Lord. He feared that he might lose, by their turning aside from the faith, what he hoped he had gained. Hence, he urged them to *"stand fast."* Earlier, he had expressed his conviction that He who had begun a good work in them would perform it (Philippians 1:6), but his intense love made him exhort them to *"stand fast in the Lord, my dearly beloved."* In such exhortations, perseverance to the end is promoted and secured.

Paul had fought bravely, and in the case of the Philippian converts, he believed that he had secured the victory, but he feared that it might yet be lost. His words remind me of the death of the British hero, General James Wolfe, who received a fatal wound while commanding his troops from the heights of Quebec, just at the moment when the enemy had begun to flee. When he knew that they were running, a smile was on his face, and he cried, "Hold me up. Let not my brave soldiers see me drop. The day is ours. Oh, do keep it!" His sole anxiety was to make the victory sure. Thus warriors die, and thus Paul lived. His very soul seemed to cry, "We have won the day. Oh, do keep it!"

My beloved, I believe that many of you are *"in the Lord,"* but I entreat you to *"stand fast in the Lord."* In your case, also, the day is won, but, oh, do keep it! That is the essence of all I am about to express to you in this chapter. May the Holy Spirit write it on your hearts!

I entreat those of you who have done all things well so far to obey the exhortation of Jude to *"keep yourselves in the love of God, looking for the mercy of our Lord Jesus Christ unto eternal life"* (Jude 1:21), and to join with me in adoring Him who alone *"is able to keep you from falling, and to present you faultless before the presence of his glory with exceeding joy"* (v. 24). Unto Him be glory forever.

In developing my thoughts on this blessed Scripture passage, I will endeavor to show you certain truths that can easily be discerned. First, it seems to me from the text that Paul perceived that these Philippian Christians were in right relationship with Christ—they were *"in the Lord"*—and in such a position that he could safely bid them to *"stand fast."*

Second, he longed that they should maintain their position: *"Stand fast in the Lord, my dearly beloved."* Moreover, he urged them to have the best motives for holding their positions. Finally, I will discuss these motives, which are found in the first two verses of our text.

Start in Right Relationship with Christ

Paul joyfully perceived that his beloved converts were in right relationship with Christ. Indeed, it is very important that we begin well. The beginning is not everything, but it is a great deal. A well-known proverb states, "Well begun is half done." That is certainly so in the things of God. It is vital to *"enter...in at the strait gate"* (Matthew 7:13) and to start on the heavenly journey from the right point.

I have no doubt that many slips and falls and apostasies of those professing to be true believers are due to the fact that they were not right at the first. Their foundations were always upon the sand (see Matthew 7:26–27). So, it was no more than might have been expected when their houses fell down at last. A flaw in the foundation is pretty sure to be followed by a crack in the superstructure. Do see to it that you lay *"a good foundation against the time to come"* (1 Timothy 6:19). It is better to have no repentance than a repentance that needs to be repented of. It is better to have no faith than a false faith. It is better to make no profession of belief than to make an untruthful one.

May God give us grace that we may not make a mistake in learning the alphabet of godliness, lest in all our learning we continue to blunder and increase in error. We should learn early the difference between grace and merit, between the purpose of God and the will of man, between trust in God and confidence in the flesh. If we do not start correctly, the farther we go, the farther we will be from our desired end, and the more thoroughly in the wrong we will find ourselves. Yes, it is of prime importance that our new birth and our first love should be genuine beyond all question.

The only position, however, in which we can begin correctly is to be *"in the Lord."* The essential point is that this is the only place to begin from which we may safely proceed. It is a very good thing for Christians to be in the church. However, if you are in the church before you are *"in the Lord,"* you are out of place. It is a good thing to be engaged in holy work. But, if you are doing holy work before you are *"in the Lord,"* you will have no heart for it, and neither will the Lord accept it. It is not essential that you be in this church or in that church, but it is essential that you be *"in the Lord."* It is not essential that you attend Sunday school or prayer meetings or the missionary society, but it is absolutely essential that you are *"in the Lord."* Paul rejoiced over those who at Philippi were converted because he knew that they were in the Lord. They were where he desired them to remain. Thus, he urged them, *"Stand fast in the Lord."*

What does it mean to be *"in the Lord"*? Well, beloved, we are in the Lord vitally and certainly when we come to the Lord Jesus by repentance and faith and make Him our refuge and hiding place. Is it so with you? Have you fled from self? Are you trusting in the Lord alone? Have you come to Calvary and beheld your Savior? As the doves build their nests in the rock, have you likewise made your home in Jesus? There is no shelter for a guilty soul but in His wounded side. Have you come there? Are you in Him? Then stay there. You will never have a better refuge. In fact, there is no other. *"Neither is there salvation in any other: for there is none other name under heaven given among men, whereby we must be saved"* (Acts 4:12).

I cannot tell you to *"stand fast in the Lord"* unless you are in Him. Hence, my first inquiry is, Are you in Christ? Is He your only confidence? In His life, His death, and His resurrection do you find the grounds of your hope? Is He Himself all your salvation and all your desire? If so, *"stand fast in the Lord."*

In Daily Living

The Philippians, in addition to having fled to Christ for refuge, were now in Christ as to their daily lives. They had heard Him say, *"Abide in me"* (John 15:4), and therefore they remained in the daily enjoyment of Him, in reliance upon Him, in obedience to Him, and in the earnest imitation of His example. They were Christians, that is to say, persons who were identified with the name of Christ. They were endeavoring to realize the power of His death and resurrection as a sanctifying influence, killing their sins and fostering their virtues. They were laboring to reproduce His image in themselves, so that they might bring glory to His name. Their lives were spent within the circle of their Savior's influence.

Are you living as they lived, my dear friends? Then stand fast. You will never find a nobler example. You will never be saturated with a more divine spirit than that of Christ Jesus your Lord. Whatever you eat or drink, or *"whatsoever ye do in word or deed, do all in the name of the Lord Jesus"* (Colossians 3:17), and so live in Him.

In Vital Union with Christ

Moreover, the Philippian believers had realized that they were in Christ by a real and vital union with Him. They had come to feel, not like separated individuals copying a model, but as members of a body, made like their Head. By a living, loving, lasting union they were joined to Christ as their Covenant Head. They could say,

> 38 *For I am persuaded, that neither death, nor life, nor angels, nor principalities, nor powers, nor things present, nor things to come,*
> 39 *Nor height, nor depth, nor any other creature, shall be able to separate us from the love of God, which is in Christ Jesus our Lord.* (Romans 8:38–39)

Do you know what it is to experience that the life in you is first in Christ and flows from Him into you, even as the life of the branch is mainly in the stem? *"I live; yet not I, but Christ liveth in me"* (Galatians 2:20). This is what it is to be in Christ. Are you in Him in this sense? Forgive my pressing the question. If your answer is in the affirmative, I entreat you to *"stand fast"* in Him. It is in Him, and in Him only, that spiritual life is to be sustained, even as only from Him can it be received. To be engrafted into Christ is salvation. To abide in Christ is the full enjoyment of it. True union with Christ is eternal life. Paul, therefore, rejoiced over these Philippians, because they were joined to the Lord in one spirit.

Christ, Our Element

The next expression, *"in the Lord,"* is very short, but very full of meaning. Does it not mean that we are in Christ as the birds are in the air, which buoys them up and enables them to fly? Are we not in Christ as the fish are in the sea? Our Lord has become our element, vital and all-surrounding. *"In him we live, and move, and have our being"* (Acts 17:28). He is in us, and we are in Him. We are *"filled with all the fulness of God"* (Ephesians 3:19), because in Christ dwells *"all the fulness of the Godhead bodily"* (Colossians 2:9), and we dwell in Him. Christ to us is all, He is in all, and He is all in all! To us, Jesus is everything in everything. Without Him we can do nothing (John 15:5), and we are nothing. Thus we are emphatically in Him. If you have attained this kind of relationship, *"stand fast"* in it.

If you dwell in the secret place of the tabernacle of the Most High, abide under the shadow of the Almighty (Psalm 91:1). Do you sit at His table and eat of His banquet? Then prolong the visit, and do not think about leaving. Say in your soul:

> Here would I find a settled rest,
> While others go and come;
> No more a stranger, or a guest,
> But like a child at home.

Has Jesus brought you into His green pastures? Then lie down in them (Psalm 23:2). Go no further, for you will never fare better. Stay with your Lord, however long the night, for only in Him do you have hope of morning.

You see, then, that these people were where they should be, *"in the Lord,"* and that this was the reason why the apostle Paul took such delight in them. See how he loved them and rejoiced over them: *"Therefore, my brethren, dearly beloved and longed for, my joy and crown, so stand fast in the Lord, my dearly beloved."* He heaped titles of love on them! Some dip their morsels in vinegar, but Paul's words were saturated with honey. Here, we not only have sweet words, but they also mean something. His love was real and fervent. Paul's heart is spelled out plainly in this verse.

Spiritual Family

Because they were in Christ, they therefore were Paul's *"brethren."* This was a new relationship, not earthly, but heavenly. What did this Jew from Tarsus know about the Philippians? Many of them were Gentiles. There had been a time when he would have called them dogs and despised them as the uncircumcised, but now he addressed them as *"my brethren."*

Lately, that poor word has become very hackneyed. We talk of "our brethren" without particularly having much brotherly love for them. True brothers have a love for one another that is very unselfish and admirable. Thus, a brotherhood exists between real Christians that they will neither disown nor dissemble nor forget. Scripture says of our Lord:

> [11] *For both he that sanctifieth and they who are sanctified are all of one: for which cause he is not ashamed to call them brethren.* (Hebrews 2:11)

Surely, therefore, believers should never be ashamed to call one another brethren. Paul, at any rate, looked at the jailer, the jailer who had set his feet in the stocks, and he looked at the jailer's family, at Lydia, and many others—

in fact, at the whole company that he had gathered at Philippi—and saluted them lovingly as *"my brethren."* Their names were written in the same family register because they were in Christ, and therefore had one Father in heaven.

Dearly Beloved

Next, Paul called them, *"my dearly beloved."* Philippians 4:1 nearly begins with these words, and the verse quite finishes with them. The repetition imparts the meaning of "my doubly dear ones." Such is the love that every true servant of Christ will have for those who have been begotten into the faith of Christ by the servant's ministry. Yes, if you are in Christ, His ministers love you. How could there be a lack of affection in our hearts toward you, especially if we have been the means of bringing you to Jesus? Without hypocrisy or display, we call you our *"dearly beloved."*

Longed For

Then, the apostle called them his *"longed for,"* that is, his most desired ones. He first desired to see them converted. After that, he desired to see them baptized. Then, he desired to see them exhibiting all the graces of Christians. When Paul saw holiness in them, he longed to visit and commune with them. Their constant kindness created in him a strong desire to speak with them face to face. He loved them and longed for their company because they were in Christ, so he spoke of them as those for whom he yearned. His delight was in thinking of them and in hoping to visit them.

A Joy and Crown

Following this, Paul called them *"my joy and crown."* Paul had been the means of their salvation. When he thought of that blessed result, he never regretted all that he had suffered. His persecutions among the Gentiles seemed light indeed, since these priceless souls were his reward. Although he was nothing but a poor prisoner of Christ, he talked in a royal style— to him they were his crown.

To Paul, the Philippians were his *stephanos*, which in Greek customs was a special crown given as an honored prize in the public games. Among the Greeks this was usually a wreath of flowers placed around the victor's brow. Paul's crown would never fade. He wrote as if he felt the never-fading amaranth on his temples. Even then, he viewed the Philippians as his wreath of honor. They were his joy and his crown. He anticipated, I do not doubt, that throughout eternity it would be a part of his heaven to see them amid their blessedness and to know that he helped to bring them to that bliss by leading them to Christ.

Beloved, it is indeed the highest joy of an ambassador for Christ that he has *"not run in vain, neither laboured in vain"* (Philippians 2:16). You who *"were as a firebrand plucked out of the burning"* (Amos 4:11) and are now living to the praise of our Lord Jesus Christ, you are the prize, the crown, the joy, of the one who was instrumental in bringing you to Christ.

Stay in Right Relationship

These converts were all this to Paul simply because they were *"in Christ."* They had begun well, they were where they should be, and so he rejoiced in them. For this reason Paul longed that they would stay there, so he exhorted them to remain where they were: *"So stand fast in the Lord, my dearly beloved."*

The beginning of faith is not the whole of it. You must not suppose that the sum of the Christian life is contained within the experience of a day or two, or a week, or a few months, or even a few years. Precious are the feelings that attend conversion, but do not dream that repentance, faith, and so forth, are just for a season, and then all is over and done with. I fear there are some who secretly think, "Everything is now complete. I have experienced the necessary change; I have been to see the elders and the pastor; I have been baptized and received into the church. Thus, everything with me is right forever." That is a false view of your condition.

Finish the Course

In conversion you have started the race, and you must run to the end of the course. In your confession of Christ, you have carried your tools into the vineyard, but the day's work now begins. Remember that *"he that shall endure unto the end, the same shall be saved"* (Matthew 24:13).

Godliness is a lifelong business. It is not a matter for a certain number of hours or for a limited period of life that we are to work out the salvation that the Lord is working in us. (See Philippians 2:12–13.) Salvation is unfolded throughout our entire sojourn here. We continue to repent and to believe, and even the process of our salvation continues as we are changed more and more into the image of our

Lord. (See 2 Corinthians 3:18.) Enduring perseverance throughout the life span is the necessary evidence of genuine conversion.

As ministers rejoice over converts, we likewise feel an intense sorrow when any disappoint us and turn out to be merely temporary camp followers. We sigh over the seed that sprang up so speedily but that withered so soon because it had neither root nor depth. (See Matthew 13:20–21.) We were ready to say, "Ring the bells of heaven," but the bells of heaven did not chime because these people talked about Christ and said they were in Christ, but it was all a delusion. After a while, for one reason and another, they turned back to their old ways.

> [19] *They went out from us, but they were not of us; for if they had been of us, they would no doubt have continued with us: but they went out, that they might be made manifest that they were not all of us.* (1 John 2:19)

Our churches suffer most seriously from the great numbers who drop out of their ranks. They either go back to the world or else must be pursuing a very secret and solitary path on their way to heaven, for we hear no more of them. Our joy is turned to disappointment, our crown of laurel becomes a circle of decaying leaves, and we are sorrowful at the remembrance of it. With great earnestness, therefore, we exhort you who are beginning the race: "Continue on your course. Neither turn aside nor slacken your running until you have won the prize."

I heard an expression recently that pleased me very much. I had spoken about the difficulty of keeping in the faith. "Yes," answered my friend, "and it is harder still to keep on keeping on." So it is. There is the hitch. I know lots of fellows who are wonders at the outset. With what a rush they start! But, there is no staying power in them. They soon lose their breath.

The difference between the spurious and the real Christian lies in his ability to stay on the course. The real Christian has a life within him that can never die, an incorruptible seed that lives and abides forever (1 Peter 1:23). In contrast, the spurious Christian starts the same, but stops almost as soon as he begins. He is esteemed as a saint, but he turns out to be a hypocrite. He makes a show for awhile, but soon he quits the way of holiness and makes his own damnation sure. God save you, dear ones, from anything that looks like apostasy. Hence, I press upon you these two weighty words: *"Stand fast."*

The Watchword for Today

Hold to the Essential Doctrines

I exhort you to stand fast doctrinally. In this age all the ships in the waters are pulling up their anchors; they are drifting with the tide; they are driven about by every wind. It is wisdom to put down more anchors. I have taken the precaution for myself to cast four anchors out of the stern, as well as to see that the great Anchor at the bow of the ship is in its proper place. I will not budge an inch from the essential doctrines for any man.

Now that the cyclone is triumphant over many a crumbling wall and tottering fence, those who are built upon the one sure Foundation (see 1 Corinthians 3:11) must prove its value by standing fast. We will hearken to no teaching but that of the Lord Jesus. If you see a truth in God's Word, grasp it by your faith. Even if it is unpopular, fasten it to you with hooks of steel. If you are despised as a fool for holding it, grasp it more firmly. Like an oak, take deeper root, because the winds would tear you from your place. Defy reproach and ridicule, and you will have already vanquished it.

"Stand fast," as the British squadrons did in prior times. When fierce assaults were made upon them, every man seemed to have been transformed into rock. In more gleeful times we might have wandered a little from the ranks to look after the fascinating flowers that grow on every side of our march. However, now that we know the Enemy surrounds us, we must keep strictly to the line of march and tolerate no roaming. The watchword of the host of God in these times is, *"Stand fast."* *"Earnestly contend for the faith which was once delivered unto the saints"* (Jude 1:3). Hold fast to sound words, and deviate not one iota from there. Doctrinally, stand fast!

Stand Fast Practically

Practically, also, abide firm in the right, the true, the holy. This is of the utmost importance. The barriers have been broken down. Some want to intermix the church and the world—yes, even the church and the theater. It has been proposed to prostitute God with the Devil in one service. Christ and Belial are to perform on one stage. Surely, now is the time when *"the lion shall eat straw like the ox"* (Isaiah 11:7), and very dirty straw, too.

I caution you: *"Come out from among them, and be ye separate, saith the Lord, and touch not the unclean thing"* (2 Corinthians 6:17). Write *"HOLINESS UNTO THE LORD"* (Zechariah 14:20) not only on your altars, but upon the bells of the horses. Let everything be done as before the living God. Do all things in holiness and edification. Strive together to maintain the purity of the disciples of Christ, take up your cross, and *"go forth...unto him without the camp, bearing his reproach"* (Hebrews 13:13).

If you have already stood apart in your decision for the Lord, continue to do so. *"Stand fast."* In nothing be moved by the laxity of the age or affected by the current of modern opinion. Just say to yourself, "I will do as Christ bids me, to the utmost of my ability. I will follow the Lamb wherever He leads." In these times of worldliness, impurity, self-indulgence, and error, the Christian is wise to roll up his pant legs and keep his feet and his clothes clean from the pollution that lies all around him. We must be more particular and precise than we have been. Oh, for grace to *"stand fast"*!

Stand Fast Experientially

Also, you need to stand fast as to your experience. Pray that your inward encounter may be a close attachment to your Master. Do not go astray from His presence. Neither climb with those who dream of perfection in the flesh, nor grovel with those who doubt the possibility of present salvation. Take Jesus Christ to be your sole treasure, and let your heart be ever with Him. Stand fast in faith in His Atonement, in confidence in His divinity, and in assurance of His Second Advent.

I yearn to know in my soul *"the power of his resurrection"* (Philippians 3:10) and to have unbroken fellowship with Him, even in sharing His sufferings. In communion with the Father, the Son, and the Holy Spirit, let us *"stand fast."* The person whose heart and soul, affections and understanding, are totally wrapped up in Christ Jesus will fare well. Concerning your inward life, your secret prayer, your walk with God, here is the watchword of the day: *"Stand fast."*

Stand Fast with Complete Trust

To put it very plainly, *"Stand fast in the Lord,"* without looking for another source to trust. Do not desire to have any hope but that which is in Christ. Do not entertain the proposition that you should unite another confidence to your confidence in the Lord. Have no hankering for any other kind of faith except the faith of a sinner in his Savior. All hope but that which is set before us in the Gospel and brought to us by the Lord Jesus is a poisoned delicacy, highly flavored, but by no means to be so much as tasted by those who have been fed the bread of heaven.

What do we need other than Jesus? What way of salvation do we seek but that of grace? What security do we have but the precious blood? *"Stand fast,"* and wish for no other *"rock of our salvation"* (Psalm 95:1) except the Lord Jesus.

Stand Fast Unwaveringly

Next, stand fast without wavering. Permit no doubt to worry you. Know that Jesus can save you, and, even more, know that He has saved you. Commit yourself totally into His hands, so that you may be as sure of your salvation as of your existence. This day *"the blood of Jesus Christ his Son cleanseth us from all sin"* (1 John 1:7). His righteousness covers us, and His life quickens us unto *"newness of life"* (Romans 6:4). Tolerate no suspicion, mistrust, doubt, or misgiving. Believe in the Lord Jesus Christ completely.

As for myself, I will yield to be lost forever if Jesus does not save me. I will have no other string to my bow, no second door of hope or way of retreat. I could risk a thousand souls on my Lord's truth and feel no risk. Stand fast, without wavering in the trust you have.

Stand Fast in Purity

Moreover, stand fast without wandering into sin. You are tempted this way and that way, but *"stand fast."* Inward passions rise. Lusts of the flesh rebel. The Devil hurls his fearful suggestions. The people of your own household tempt you. Nevertheless, *"stand fast."* Only in this way will you be preserved from the torrents of iniquity. Keep close to the example and spirit of your Master, and *"having done all,* [still] *stand"* (Ephesians 6:13).

Stand Fast Tirelessly

As I have exhorted you to stand fast without wandering, so next I must encourage you to stand fast without growing weary. (See 2 Thessalonians 3:13.) You are tired. Never mind. Take a little rest and brush up again. You say, "this toil is so monotonous." Do it better, and that will be a change. Your Savior endured His life and labor without this complaint, for zeal had consumed Him (John 2:17). "Alas!" you cry, "I cannot see results." Never mind. Wait for results, even as the husbandman waits for the precious fruits of the earth. "I plod along and make no progress," you say. Never mind. You are a poor judge of your own success. Work on, for *"in due reason we shall reap, if we faint not"* (Galatians 6:9).

Practice perseverance. Remember that if you have the work of faith and the labor of love, you must complete the trio with the addition of the patience of hope. (See 1 Thessalonians 1:3.) You cannot go on without this last thing.

> [58] *Therefore, my beloved brethren, be ye stedfast, unmoveable, always abounding in the work of the Lord, forasmuch as ye know that your labour is not in vain in the Lord.* (1 Corinthians 15:58)

I am reminded of Sir Christopher Wren, the great English architect, when he cleared away old St. Paul's to make room for his splendid new edifice. He was compelled to use battering rams against the massive walls. The workmen kept on battering and battering. An enormous force was brought to bear on the walls for many days and nights, but it did not appear to have made the least impression on the ancient masonry. Yet, the wise architect knew what he was doing. He instructed the workmen to keep on incessantly. Thus, the ram fell again and again against the rocky wall until, at length, the whole mass was disintegrating and coming apart. Then, the results of each stroke began to show. At one blow it reeled, at another it quivered, with the next it moved visibly, and with the final impact it fell over amid clouds of dust. Do you think these last strokes did all the work? No, it was the combination of blows, the first as truly as the last. Keep on with the battering ram.

I hope to keep on until I die. Mark you, I may die without seeing the errors of the hour totter and fall, but I will be perfectly content to sleep in Christ, for I have a sure expectation that this work will succeed in the end. I will be happy to have done my share, even if I personally see little apparent results.

Lord, let Your unseen work be apparent to Your servants, and we will be content that Your glory should be reserved for our children. *"Stand fast,"* my beloved, in incessant labors, for the results are sure.

Stand Fast without Distortion

In addition to standing fast tirelessly, stand fast without allowing your faith to become distorted. Timber, when it is rather green, is apt to bend this way or that. The spiritual weather is very bad just now for green wood. One day it is damp with superstition; another it is parched with skepticism. Rationalism and ritualism are both at work. I pray that you may not warp. Keep straight. Keep to the truth, the whole truth, and nothing but the truth, for in the Master's name we bid you, *"Stand fast in the Lord."*

"Stand fast," for there is great need. *"Many walk, of whom I have told you often, and now tell you even weeping, that they are the enemies of the cross of Christ"* (Philippians 3:18).

Strive to Stand Fast

Paul urged the saints at Philippi to stand fast because, even in his own case, spiritual life was a struggle. Paul had written to them, *"Not as though I had already attained, either were already perfect"* (Philippians 3:12). He was pressing forward. He was straining with all of his energy by the power of the Holy Spirit. He did not expect to be carried to heaven on a feather bed. He was warring and agonizing. You, beloved, must do the same.

What a grand example of perseverance Paul set for us all! Nothing enticed him from his steadfastness. *"None of these things move me, neither count I my life dear unto myself"* (Acts 20:24). He has entered into his rest, because the Lord his God helped him to maintain his stance to the end. Most earnestly, from the depths of my soul, I implore you with this: *"Stand fast in the Lord, my dearly beloved."*

The Best Motivation for Standing Fast

Paul also urged the Philippians to have the right reasons for standing fast. He knew that no matter how their behavior appeared to others, *"man looketh on the outward appearance, but the LORD looketh on the heart"* (1 Samuel 16:7). Further, he was concerned that they follow the biblical mandate that *"whatsoever ye do, do all to the glory of God"* (1 Corinthians 10:31) and not for personal, fleshly motives.

Heavenly Citizenship

First of all, Paul urged them to stand fast because of their citizenship: *"For our citizenship is in heaven"* (Philippians 3:20 RV). If you are in Christ, you are citizens of the New Jerusalem. (See Revelation 3:12.) Men ought to behave themselves according to their citizenship and not dishonor their country.

When a man was a citizen of ancient Athens, he felt it incumbent upon him to be brave. Xerxes[1] said, "These Athenians are not ruled by kings; how will they fight?" "No, they are

---

[1] Xerxes the Great, king of Persia from 486–465 B.C.

not," the reply came, "but every man respects the law, and each man is ready to die for his country."

Xerxes soon learned that the same obedience and respect of law ruled the Spartans, and that they, because they were of Sparta, were all brave as lions. He sent word to Leonidas[2] and his little troop to give up their arms. "Come and take them" was the courageous reply. The Persian king had myriads of soldiers with him, while Leonidas had only three hundred Spartans at his side. Yet, the Spartans held the pass. It cost the Persian despot many thousands of men to force a passage. The sons of Sparta died rather than desert their post. Every citizen of Sparta felt that he must stand fast: it was not for such a man as he to yield.

I like the spirit of Bayard, that sixteenth century French knight who was without fear and without reproach. He did not know what fear meant. In his last battle, his spine was broken, and he said to those around him, "Place me up against a tree, so that I may sit up and die with my face to the enemy."

Yes, if our backs were broken, if we could no more bear the shield or use the sword, it would be incumbent upon us, as citizens of the

---

[2] Leonidas: Greek hero, king of Sparta from around 490–480 B.C.

New Jerusalem, to die with our faces toward the Enemy. We must not yield, we dare not yield, if we are of *"the city of the great King"* (Psalm 48:2). The martyrs urge us to stand fast; the *"cloud of witnesses"* (Hebrews 12:1), bending from their thrones above, beseech us to stand fast; all the shining, heavenly hosts cry to us, *"Stand fast."* Stand fast for God, the truth, and holiness, and let no man take your crown.

With a View toward Christ's Return

The next matter Paul brought up was their outlook. *"Our conversation is in heaven; from whence also we look for the Saviour, the Lord Jesus Christ."* Beloved, Jesus is coming. He is even now on the way. You have heard the tidings until you scarcely give them credence; but the word is true, and it will surely be fulfilled before long. The Lord is coming indeed. He promised to come to die, and He kept His word. He now promises to come to reign, and you can be sure that He will keep His trust with His people. He is coming. Ears of faith can hear the sound of His chariot wheels approaching. Every moment of time and every event of providence bring Him nearer. Blessed will be those servants who are not sleeping when He returns, nor who are wandering from their posts of duty. Happy will they be whom the Lord finds faithfully watching and standing fast in that Last Day. (See Luke 12:37.)

To us, beloved, Christ is coming, not as Judge and Destroyer, but as Savior. We look for the Savior, the Lord Jesus Christ. Now, if we do look for Him, let us *"stand fast."* There must be no going into sin, no forsaking the fellowship of the church, no leaving the truth, no trying to play fast and loose with godliness, no running with the hares and hunting with the hounds. Let us stand so fast in singleness of heart that, whenever Jesus comes, we can joyously cry, "Welcome, welcome, Son of God!"

Sometimes I wait through the weary years with great comfort. There was a ship some time ago outside a certain harbor. A heavy sea made the ship roll fearfully. A dense fog blotted out all buoys and lights. The captain never left the wheel. He could not make his way into the harbor, and for a long time no pilot could get out to him from the harbor. Eager passengers urged him to be courageous and make a dash for the harbor. He said, "No, it is not my duty to run so great a risk. A pilot is required here, and I will wait for one if I wait a week."

The truest courage is that which can bear to be charged with cowardice. To wait is much wiser than to steam on and wreck your vessel on the rocks when you cannot hear the foghorn and have no pilot. Our prudent captain waited his time, and at last he spied the pilot's boat coming to him over the turbulent sea. When the pilot went to work, the captain's anxious waiting was over.

The church is like that vessel, pitched to and fro in the dark storm, and the pilot has not yet come. The weather is very threatening. All around, the darkness hangs like a pall, but Jesus will come before long, walking on the water. He will bring us safely to the desired haven. Let us wait with patience. *"Stand fast."* Jesus is coming, and in Him is our sure hope.

Great Expectations

Further, Paul supplied another true motive, an expectation. *"Christ...shall change our vile body,"* or literally, "the body of our humiliation." Think of it, dear friends! No more headaches or heartaches, no more feebleness and fainting, no more inner tumors or tuberculosis. Rather, the Lord will transfigure this body of humiliation into the likeness of the body of His glory.

Our frames are now made up of decaying substances. These bodies are *"of the earth, earthy"* (1 Corinthians 15:47). Our bodies groan, suffer, become diseased, and die. Blessed be God, we will be wonderfully changed, and then *"there shall be no more death, neither sorrow, nor crying, neither shall there be any more pain"* (Revelation 21:4).

The natural appetites of this body engender sad tendencies to sin, and in this respect it is a *"vile body."* It will not always be so. The great change will deliver it from all that is unseemly and carnal. It will be as pure as the Lord's body! Whatever the body of Christ is now, our bodies will be like it. After His resurrection, He said to His disciples, *"Handle me, and see; for a spirit hath not flesh and bones, as ye see me have"* (Luke 24:39). Each of us will have a real, corporeal body, just as Christ's body now has physical substance. Like His body, it will be full of beauty, full of health and strength. It will enjoy unique immunities from evil and special adaptations for good. That is what is going to happen to us.

Therefore, let us stand firm in our belief, *"which is Christ in you, the hope of glory"* (Colossians 1:27). Let us not willingly throw away our prospects of glory and immortality. What! Relinquish resurrection and glory? Relinquish likeness to the risen Lord? O God, save us from such terrible apostasy! Save us from such immeasurable folly! Do not allow us to retreat in the day of battle, since that would be to turn our backs away from the crown of glory that does not fade away (1 Peter 5:4).

Vast Resources of Strength

The apostle Paul then urged the Philippians (and us) to stand fast because of our resources in Christ. Someone may ask, "How can this body of yours be transformed and transfigured so that it becomes like the body of Christ?" I cannot tell you anything about the process. It will all be accomplished *"in a moment, in the twinkling of an eye, at the last trump"* (1 Corinthians 15:52). But, I can tell you by what power it will be accomplished. The omnipotent Lord will bare His arm and exercise His might, *"according to the working whereby he is able even to subdue all things unto himself."*

Beloved, we may well stand fast, since we have infinite power backing us. The Lord is with us with all His energy, even with His all-conquering strength, which will yet subdue all His foes. Do not imagine that any enemy can be too strong for Christ's arm. Since *"he is able even to subdue all things unto himself,"* He can certainly bear us through all opposition. A single glance of His eye may wither all opposers, or, better still, one word from His lips may turn them into friends.

The army of the Lord is strong in reserves. These reserves have never yet been fully called out. We who are in the field are only a small squadron, holding the fort, but our Lord has at His back ten thousand times ten thousand who will carry war into the Enemy's camp. When the Captain of Salvation comes to the front, He will bring His heavenly legions with Him. Our business is to watch until He appears upon the scene. (See Matthew 24:42.) When He comes, His infinite resources will be put in marching order.

I like that speech of Wellington[3] (who was so calm amid the roar of Waterloo), when an officer had sent this word: "Tell the Commander in Chief that he must move me. I cannot hold my position any longer, because my numbers have been so thinned." The great general replied, "Tell him he must hold his place. Every Englishman today must die where he stands or else win the victory." The officer read the command to hold his position, and he did stand until the trumpet sounded victory.

So it is with us now. My fellow soldiers, we must die where we are rather than yield to the

---

[3] Wellington: Arthur Wellesley (1769–1852), British general and statesman, first Duke of Wellington.

Enemy. If Jesus tarries, we must not desert our posts. Wellington knew that the heads of the Prussian columns would soon be visible, coming in to ensure the victory. Likewise, by faith we can perceive the legions of our Lord approaching. In staggered ranks, His angels fly through as the heavens open. The air is teeming with them. I hear their silver trumpets. Behold, He comes with clouds! When He comes, He will abundantly recompense all who have stood fast amid the raging battle.

Chapter Four

The Final Judgment

*For we must all appear before the judgment
seat of Christ; that every one may receive
the things done in his body,
according to that he hath done,
whether it be good or bad.
—2 Corinthians 5:10*

I now want to address what follows immediately after the resurrection of the dead, namely, the final Judgment. The dead will be raised on purpose, so that they may be judged in their bodies. Their resurrection will be the immediate prelude to the Judgment.

There is no need for me to try to prove to you from Scripture that this great Judgment will occur, for the Word of God abounds with passages that reveal this truth. You find them throughout the Old Testament. The psalmists anticipated that great Judgment in the Psalms (especially in Psalms 9, 49, 50, 72, 96–98, and 110), for most assuredly the Lord is coming again. *"And he shall judge the world in righteousness, he shall minister judgment to the people in uprightness"* (Psalm 9:8). Because God will judge every secret thing, Solomon issued this very solemn, yet tender warning:

> [9] *Rejoice, O young man, in thy youth; and let thy heart cheer thee in the days of thy youth, and walk in the ways of thine heart, and in the sight of thine eyes: but know thou, that for all these things God will bring thee into judgment.*
>
> (Ecclesiastes 11:9)

In night visions Daniel beheld the Son of Man coming with the clouds of heaven and drawing near to the Ancient of Days. Then he saw that the Messiah was given everlasting dominion over all, and the nations gathered before Him to be judged. (See Daniel 7:13–14.) This was no new doctrine to the Jews. It was received and accepted by them as a most certain fact that there would be a Day in which God would judge the earth in righteousness.

The New Testament is very expressive about the coming Judgment. The twenty-fifth chapter of Matthew contains language, from the lips of the Savior Himself, that could not possibly be more clear and definite:

> ³¹ *When the Son of man shall come in his glory, and all the holy angels with him, then shall he sit upon the throne of his glory:*
> ³² *And before him shall be gathered all nations: and he shall separate them one from another, as a shepherd divideth his sheep from the goats:*
> ³³ *And he shall set the sheep on his right hand, but the goats on the left.*
> ³⁴ *Then shall the King say unto them on his right hand, Come, ye blessed of my Father, inherit the kingdom prepared for you from the foundation of the world....*
> ⁴¹ *Then shall he say also unto them on the left hand, Depart from me, ye cursed, into everlasting fire, prepared for the devil and his angels....*
> ⁴⁶ *And these shall go away into everlasting punishment: but the righteous into life eternal.* (Matthew 25:31–34, 41, 46)

"Jesus Christ, who is the faithful witness" (Revelation 1:5), *"will not lie"* (Proverbs 14:5). He said that all nations will gather before Him, and He will divide them one from the other, as a shepherd divides the sheep from the goats.

An abundance of other New Testament passages are plain enough. One that I will quote is the entire passage containing our text verse, found in the apostle Paul's second letter to the Thessalonians:

> [7] *And to you who are troubled rest with us, when the Lord Jesus shall be revealed from heaven with his mighty angels,*
> [8] *In flaming fire taking vengeance on them that know not God, and that obey not the gospel of our Lord Jesus Christ:*
> [9] *Who shall be punished with everlasting destruction from the presence of the Lord, and from the glory of his power;*
> [10] *When he shall come to be glorified in his saints, and to be admired in all them that believe (because our testimony among you was believed) in that day.*
>
> (2 Thessalonians 1:7–10)

As we discovered in a previous chapter, Revelation is very graphic in its depiction of the Judgment. The prophet of Patmos wrote:

> [11] *And I saw a great white throne, and him that sat on it, from whose face the earth and the heaven fled away; and there was found no place for them.*
> [12] *And I saw the dead, small and great, stand before God; and the books were opened: and another book was opened, which is the book of life: and the dead were judged out of those things which were written in the books, according to their works.* (Revelation 20:11–12)

Space would fail me if I referred you to all the Scriptures that point to the Judgment. You will find that the Holy Spirit, whose word is truth (John 17:17), repeatedly has asserted that the great Judgment of *"the quick and the dead"* (2 Timothy 4:1; 1 Peter 4:5) will occur.

Besides that direct testimony, it should be remembered there is a cogent argument that it must occur because God, as the Ruler over men, is absolutely just. In all human governments, courts of justice must exist. Government cannot be conducted without its days of session and of trial. Thus, inasmuch as sin and evil are clearly in this world, it might fairly be anticipated that there will be a time when God will sit on the judgment seat. Then He will call the prisoners before Him, and the guilty will receive their condemnation.

But, decide for yourselves: Is this present state the conclusion of all things? If so, what evidence would you cite of divine justice, in face of the fact that the best of men in this world are often the poorest and most afflicted, while the worst acquire wealth, practice oppression, and receive the crowd's homage? Who are they who *"ride upon the high places of the earth"* (Isaiah 58:14)? They must be those who

Wade through slaughter to a throne
And shut the gates of mercy on mankind.

Where are the servants of God? They are in obscurity and often suffering. Do they not sit like Job among the ashes, subjects of little pity, objects of much upbraiding? And where are the enemies of God? Are not many of them *"clothed in purple and fine linen and* [faring] *sumptuously every day"* (Luke 16:19)? If there is no hereafter, then those rich men have the best of it, and the selfish man who does not fear God, is, after all, the wisest of men and more to be commended than his fellows. (See Luke 16:8–9.)

However, it cannot be so. Our common sense revolts against the thought. There must be another state in which these anomalies will all be rectified. *"If in this life only we have hope in Christ, we are of all men most miserable"* (1 Corinthians 15:19), wrote the apostle. In those times of persecution, the best of men were driven to the worst of straits for being God's servants. Would you then apply the inscription, *Finis coronat opus,* which means "the end crowns the work"? That cannot be the final issue of life, or justice itself is frustrated. There must be a restitution for those who suffer unjustly. There must be a punishment for the wicked and the oppressor.

Not only can this be affirmed from a general sense of justice, but there is also in the conscience of most men, if not of all, an assent to this fact. As an old Puritan said,

> God holds a petty session in every man's conscience, which is the earnest of the assize [judgment] which He will hold by and by; for almost all men judge themselves, and their conscience knows this to be wrong and that to be right. I say "almost all," for there seems to be in this generation a race of men who have so stultified their conscience that the spark appears to have gone out, and they put bitter for sweet and sweet for bitter. The lie they seem to approve, but the truth they do not recognize. But let conscience alone and do not stupefy her, and you shall find her bearing witness that there is a Judge of all the earth who must do right.

Now, this is truly the case when the conscience is fully active. Men who are busy with their work or entertained with their pleasures often keep their consciences quiet. As John Bunyan put it, they shut up Mr. Conscience, blind his windows, and barricade his doors. As for the great bell on the top of the house that the old gentleman loved to ring, they cut the bell rope so that he cannot get at it, for they do not wish him to disturb the town of Mansoul. But when death approaches, it often happens that Mr. Conscience escapes from his prison.

Then, I warrant you, he makes such a din that there is not a sleeping head in all of Mansoul. He cries out and avenges himself for his constrained silence, making the man know that there is a something within him that is not quite dead, which still demands justice, and that sin cannot go unchastised.

There must be a Judgment, then. The fact that Scripture asserts it should be enough to firmly establish that there will be a final Day of Judgment. But, by way of collateral evidence, we find that the natural order of things requires it and, additionally, that our consciences attest to it.

Now we come to consider what our text says about the Judgment. I pray you, beloved, if I write coldly about this momentous truth, or fail to excite your attention and stir your deepest emotions, forgive me. May God forgive me also, because I would have good reason to ask His forgiveness; this topic, above all, should arouse my zeal for the honor of the Lord and for the welfare of my fellow creatures, stirring me to be doubly in earnest. However, if ever there were a theme that did not depend on my ability to write convincingly (which alone should command your attention), it is that which I now bring before you. I feel no need of well-selected words. The mere mention of the fact that such a Judgment is impending and will occur before long might well hold you in breathless silence, arrest the throbbing of your pulse, and choke the utterance of your lips. The certainty of it, the reality of it, the terrors that accompany it, the impossibility of escaping from it, all appeal to us now and demand our vigilance.

Who Must Appear?

Now, we will explore the question, Who will have to appear before the throne of judgment? The answer in our text is plain and allows for no exemption: *"We must all appear before the judgment seat of Christ."* This is very decisive, even if there were no other reference to it. *"We must all appear,"* that is, everyone of the human race must appear. That the godly will not be exempted from this appearance is very clear, for the apostle is speaking here to Christians. He said, *"We walk by faith, not by sight"* (2 Corinthians 5:7); *"We are confident"* (v. 8); *"We labour"* (v. 9); and then, *"We must all appear."* So, disregarding all others, it is certain that all Christians must appear there. The text is quite explicit on that point.

If we did not have the Corinthian passage, we still have the one in Matthew, previously cited, in which the sheep are summoned to the judgment seat as certainly as the goats are. (See Matthew 25:31–46.) We also have the passage in Revelation 20:12–13, where all the dead are judged according to the things that are written in God's books.

Right now, someone who is reading this is probably thinking, "I thought that the sins of the righteous, having been pardoned and forever blotted out, would never come into the Judgment." May I remind you, beloved, that if they are so pardoned and blotted out—as they undoubtedly are—the righteous have no reason to fear coming into the Judgment. They are the people who covet the Judgment and will be able to stand there to receive a public acquittal from the mouth of the great Judge. Who among us wishes, as it were, to be smuggled into heaven unlawfully? Who desires to have it said by those who are damned in hell, "You were never tried, or else you might have been condemned as we were."

O beloved, we have a hope that we can stand the trial. The way of righteousness by Christ Jesus enables us to submit ourselves to the most tremendous tests, which even that burning Day will bring forth. We should not be afraid to be weighed in the scales of justice. We even desire that Day when our faith in Jesus

Christ is strong and firm. We can say, *"Who is he that condemneth?"* (Romans 8:34). We can challenge the Day of Judgment. *"Who shall lay any thing to the charge of God's elect"* (Romans 8:33) in that Day, or at any other, since Christ has died and has risen again?

It is necessary that the righteous be present so that there is not any partiality in the matter whatsoever, that the verdicts may be all clear and straight, and that the rewards of the righteous may be seen to be without any violation of the most rigorous justice, even though the rewards are all of grace.

Dearly beloved, what a Day it will be for the righteous! For some of them were—perhaps some reading this are—lying under some very terrible accusation of which they are perfectly guiltless. All will be cleared up then, and that will be one great blessing of the Judgment Day. There will be a resurrection of reputations as well as of bodies. In this world, the righteous are called fools; at the Judgment, they will *"shine forth as the sun in the kingdom of their Father"* (Matthew 13:43). Ungodly men have hounded the righteous to death as not being fit to live. In early ages they laid on Christians charges of the most terrible character, which I would be ashamed to mention, but on that Day their reputations will all be cleared.

Those *"of whom the world was not worthy"* (Hebrews 11:38), who were driven and hunted and forced to dwell in caves, will come forth as worthy ones. The world will know her true aristocracy. Earth will acknowledge her true nobility. The men whose names she cast out as evil will then be held in great repute, for they will stand out clear and transparent without spot or blemish. (See Ephesians 5:27.) It is good that there should be a trial for the righteous, for the clearing and vindication of their names, and that it should be public, defying the censure and criticism of all mankind.

"We must all appear." What a vast assembly, what a prodigious gathering—that of the entire human race! As I was meditating on this subject, I wondered what the thoughts of Father Adam will be, as he stands there with Mother Eve and looks upon his offspring. It will be the first time in which he will ever have the opportunity of seeing all his children gathered together. What a sight he will then behold—far stretching, covering all the globe that they inhabit, enough not only to populate all the earth's plains, but to crown her hilltops and cover the waves of the sea. How numberless will the human race be when all the generations that have ever lived, or will ever live, will at once rise from the dead! What a sight

that will be! Is it too marvelous for our imagination to picture?

Yet, it is quite certain that the assemblage will be mustered, and the spectacle will be beheld. Everyone from before the Flood, from the days of the Patriarchs, from the times of David, from the Babylonian kingdom, all the legions of Assyria, all the hosts of Persia, all the troops of the Greeks, all the vast armies and legions of Rome, the barbarian, the Scythian, the bond, the free (Colossians 3:11), men of every color and of every tongue—they will all stand in that Last Day before the judgment seat of Christ.

There come the kings, no greater than the men they call their slaves. There come the princes, but they have removed their coronets, for they must stand like common flesh and blood. Here come the judges to be judged themselves, and the advocates and barristers needing an advocate themselves. Here come those who thought themselves too good and kept to themselves on the street. There are the Pharisees, hustled by the publicans on either side and sunk down to the same level with them. Mark the peasants as they rise from the soil. See the teeming myriad from outside the great cities streaming in, countless hosts that not even Alexander or Napoleon ever beheld!

Observe how the servant is as great as his master. "Liberty, Equality, Fraternity," the great cry of the French Revolution, is truly proclaimed now. No kings, no princes, no nobles, can shelter themselves behind their titles, assert privileges, or claim immunity. Alike on one common level, they stand together to be tried before the last tremendous tribunal.

The wicked of every sort will come. Proud Pharaoh will be there; Senacherib, the haughty; Herod, who would have slain the young Child; Judas, who sold his Master for gold; Demas, who deserted His church for the world; and Pilate, who would gladly have washed his hands in innocence. There will come the long list of infallibles, the whole line of popes, to receive their damnation at the Almighty's hands, with the priests that trod on the necks of nations and the tyrants that used the priests as their tools. They will come to receive the thunderbolts of God that they so richly deserve. Oh, what a scene it will be! These groups, which seem to us to be so large, how they will shrink to the size of a drop in a bucket as compared with the ocean of life that will swell around the throne at the last great Judgment Day! They will all be there.

Now, to me, the most important thought connected with this is that I will be there; to you young ones, that you will be there; to you elderly, that you all will be there. Are you rich? Your finery will be cast off. Are you poor? Your rags will not exempt you from attendance. One will say, "I am too obscure." You must come out from that hiding place. Some will say, "I am too public." You must come down from that pedestal. Everyone must be at that court. Note the words *we* and *all* in *"We must all appear."*

Still further, note the word *appear* in our text. No disguise will be possible. You cannot come there dressed in the costume of vocation or attired in robes of state, but you must appear. You must be seen through, must be displayed, must be revealed. Off will come your garments, and your spirit will be judged of God, not by outward appearance, but according to the inward heart. (See 1 Samuel 16:7.) What a Day that will be when every man sees himself and his fellowman clearly, and when the eyes of angels, devils, and the Lord on the throne see him thoroughly. Let these thoughts dwell in your mind, while you take this for the answer to our first inquiry, Who is to be judged?

Who Will Judge

Our second question is, Who will be the judge? *"We must all appear before the judgment seat of Christ.*" That Christ has been appointed the Judge of all mankind is most proper and fitting. British law ordains that a man be tried by his peers. There is justice in that statute. Likewise, God will judge men, but at the same time it will be in the person of Jesus Christ, the Man. Men will be judged by a man. He who was once judged by men will judge men. Jesus knows what man should be; He who is ordained to administer the law with authority was Himself *"made under the law"* (Galatians 4:4) in deep humility. He can hold the scales of justice evenly, for He stood in man's place as He bore and braved man's temptations. (See Hebrews 4:15.) He therefore is the most fit Judge.

I have sometimes heard and read sermons in which the preacher said a Christian ought to rejoice that his Friend will be his Judge. No impropriety may have been intended, but it seems to me a rather questionable suggestion. I would not put it in that way, because I believe any judge who is partial to his friends while on the judicial bench should be removed from the seat immediately. I expect no favoritism from Christ, my Judge. I do expect that when He sits there, He will dispense even-handed justice to all. I cannot see how it is right for anyone to propose that we should find encouragement in the Judge being our Friend.

Friend or no friend, every one of us will have a fair trial, because Christ is *"no respecter of persons"* (Acts 10:34). Of Him whom God has appointed to judge the world, it will not be said, when the Judgment is over, that He winked at the crimes of some and overlooked them, while He searched out the faults of others and convicted them. He will be fair and upright throughout. He is our Friend, I grant you, and He will be our Friend and Savior forever; but as our Judge, we must believe and maintain the thought that He will be impartial to all the sons of men. O man, you will have a fair trial. He who will judge you will not take sides against you.

In the past I thought that certain men have been shielded from the punishment they deserved because they were of a select clerical status or because they occupied a certain official position. A poor laborer who kills his wife is hanged, but when another man of superior station does the same deed of violence and stains his hands with the blood of her whom he had vowed to love and cherish, the capital sentence is not executed upon him.

Everywhere in the world we see that, even with the best intentions, justice somehow or other squints a little. Even in this country, there is just the slightest possible tipping of the scales. May God grant that such a distortion be cured soon. I do not think it is intentional, and I hope the nation will not have to complain about it for long. The same justice ought to exist for the poorest beggar who crawls into a filthy slum as for the titled nobleman who owns the broadest acres in all of the country.

Before the law, at least, all men ought to have an equal standing. We can rejoice that at the final Judgment it will be so with the Judge of all the earth. *Fiat justitia, ruat caelum*— "Let justice be done though the heavens fall." Christ will, by all means, hold the scales even.

You will have a fair trial and a full trial, too. There will be no concealment of anything in your favor and no keeping back of anything against you. No witnesses will be hidden across the sea to keep them out of the way. They will all be there, all testimony will be there, and all that is needed to condemn or to acquit will be produced in full court at that trial. Hence, it will be a final trial. From that court there will be no appeal. If Christ says, "Cursed!" cursed must they be forever. If Christ says, "Blessed!" blessed are they forever. Well, this is what we have to expect then, to stand before the throne of Christ Jesus, the Son of God, and there to be judged.

How Will We Be Judged?

Our third point of inquiry is, What will be the standard of the Judgment? Our text says, *"That every one may receive the things done in his body, according to that he hath done, whether it be good or bad."* Thus, it would appear that our actions will be taken as evidence; not our profession, not our boasting, but our actions will be taken as evidence, and every man will receive a just verdict according to what he has done in his body. The text implies that everything done by us in this body will be known then. It is all recorded. It will all be brought to light.

Hence, in the Day of Judgment every secret sin will be published. What was done in private, what was hidden by the darkness— every secret thing—will be published abroad. With great care you have concealed it; most cleverly you have covered it up; but it will be revealed, to your own astonishment, to form a part of the case against you.

There, hypocritical actions as well as secret sins will be laid bare. The Pharisee who devoured the widow's house and made a long prayer will find that widow's house brought against him and that long prayer, too, for the long prayer will then be understood as having been a long lie from beginning to end. Oh, how fine we can make some things look with the aid of paint and varnish and gilt! But, at the Last Day, off will come the varnish and veneer, and the true metal, the real substance, will then be seen.

When it is said that everything that is done in the body will be brought up as evidence for us or against us, remember this includes every omission as well as every commission of sin. (See James 4:17.) What was not done that should have been done is as greatly sinful as the doing of that which should not have been done. Have you ever noticed in Christ's account of the Judgment, when the sheep were separated from the goats, how those on the left were condemned, not for what they did, but for what they did not do: *"For I was an hungered, and ye gave me no meat: I was thirsty, and ye gave me no drink"* (Matthew 25:42)? According to this principle, how would some of you stand before God, you who have neglected holiness, faith, and repentance all your days? I urge you to consider your present state.

Remember, too, that all our words will be brought up: *"Every idle word that men shall speak, they shall give account thereof in the day of judgment"* (Matthew 12:36). Add to them all of our thoughts, for these lie at the bottom of our actions and give the true color to them, good or bad. Our motives, our heart sins, our neglect of the Gospel, our unbelief, and especially our hatred of Christ—all of these will be read aloud and published unreservedly.

"Well," someone says, "who then can be saved?" Indeed, who then can be saved? Let me tell you. There will come forward those who have believed in Jesus, and even though they have many sins to which they might well plead guilty, they will be able to say, "Great God, You provided a Substitute for us, and You said that if we would accept Him, He would be our Substitute and take our sins on Himself. We did accept Him, and our sins were laid on Him, and we now have no sins to be charged against us. We have been purged of them, because they were transferred from us to the great Savior, Substitute, and Sacrifice."

In that Day none will be able to express an objection to that plea. It will hold, for God has said, *"He that believeth on him is not condemned"* (John 3:18). Then, the gracious actions of the righteous will be brought forth to prove that they had faith, for the faith that never evidences itself by good works is a dead faith and a faith that will never save a soul. (See James 2:14–20.)

If someone were to object to the pardoning of the thief who died on a cross next to our Savior, the thief could say, "My sins were laid on Jesus." Satan might reply, "Yes, but what about your good works? You must have some evidence of your faith." Then the recording angel would say, "The dying thief said to his fellow thief who was dying with him, *'Dost not thou fear God?'* (Luke 23:40). In his last moments he did what he could; he rebuked the thief that was dying with him and made a good confession of his Lord. That was the evidence of the sincerity of his faith."

Friend, will there be any evidence of the sincerity of your faith? If your faith has no evidence before the Lord, what will you do? Suppose you thought you had faith and went on drinking. Suppose you went, as I know some have done, straight from church into the pubs? Or, suppose you joined a church but remained a drunkard? Women have done that as well as men and are not exempt. Suppose you professed to have faith in Christ and yet cheated in your business dealings? Do you think that God will never require justice for these things?

If you are no better than other men in your conduct, you are no better than other men in your character, and you will stand no better than other men in the Judgment Day. If your actions are not superior to theirs, then you may profess what you will about your faith, but you are deceived, and, as such, you will be discovered at the Judgment.

If grace does not differentiate us from other men, it is not the grace that God gives His elect. We are not perfect, but all of God's saints keep their eyes on the great standard of perfection and, with strong desire, aim to walk worthy of God's high calling and to bring forth works that show that they love God. If we do not have these signs following our faith, or if they are not put in as evidence for us, we will not be able to prove our faith at the Last Day.

Oh, you who have no faith in Christ, no faith in Jesus as your Substitute, that treacherous unbelief of yours will be a condemning sin against you! It will be proof positive that you hated God, because a man must hate God indeed who will spurn His counsels, give no heed to His reproof, scorn His grace, and dare the vengeance of Him who points out the way of escape and the path that leads to life. He who will not be saved by God's mercy proves that He hates the God of mercy. God gave His own Son to die to redeem men from their just condemnation. Yet, if a person will not trust in His Son and will not have Him as his Savior, then that one sin, even if he had no other, would at once prove that he was an enemy of God and black at heart.

However, if your faith is in Jesus, if you love Jesus, if your heart goes out to Jesus, if your life is influenced by Jesus, if you make Him your Example as well as your Savior, there will be evidence—you may not see it, but there will be evidence—in your favor. Notice those gracious acts that were mentioned when the evidence was brought forth by Christ:

> ³⁵ *For I was an hungered, and ye gave me meat: I was thirsty, and ye gave me drink: I was a stranger, and ye took me in:*
> ³⁶ *Naked, and ye clothed me: I was sick, and ye visited me: I was in prison, and ye came unto me.* (Matthew 25:35–36)

The righteous, for whom Christ was offering evidence, replied, "Lord, we never knew this." (See Matthew 25:37–39.)

Should anyone in my presence declare, "I have plenty of evidence to prove my faith," I would necessarily chastise him with this rebuke: "Hold your tongue! Hold your tongue! I am afraid you have no faith at all, or you would not be talking about your evidence." But, if a person says, "I am afraid I have no evidence that will stand me in good stead at the last," and yet if he had been feeding the hungry and clothing the naked and doing all he could for Christ, I would tell him not to be afraid.

The Master will find witnesses to say, "That man relieved me when I was in poverty. He knew I was one of Christ's, and he came and helped me." And another (perhaps it will be an angel) will come and say, "I saw him when he was alone and heard him pray for his enemies." And the Lord will say, "I saw his heart when he put up with rebuke and slander and persecution and would not respond, for My sake. He did it all as evidence that My grace was in his heart." You will not have to find the witnesses. The Judge will call them, for He knows all about your case.

As Christ calls the witnesses, you will be surprised to find how even the ungodly will be obliged to consent to the just salvation of the righteous. How the secret deeds of the righteous and their true sincerity of heart, when thus unveiled, will make devils bite their tongues in wrath to think that there was so much grace given to the sons of men with which to defeat persecution, to overcome temptation, and to follow on in obedience to the Lord!

Yes, the deeds of men—not their prating, not their profession, not their talk, but their deeds—will be the evidence of the grace given to them (although nobody will be saved by the merits of his deeds), or their deeds will be the evidence of their unbelief. Thus, by their works will men stand before the Lord, or by their works will they be condemned. Their deeds will be evidence for or against them, and nothing more.

What Will Result?

Our last point of inquiry is, What will the consequences of this Judgment be? Will sentences of acquittal and condemnation be handed down, and then the whole thing be over? Far from it! The Judgment will occur with a view toward what follows: *"That every one may receive the things done in his body."* The Lord will grant to His people an abundant reward for all that they have done, not that they deserve any reward. God first gave them grace to do good works, then He took their good works as evidence of a renewed heart, and next He will give them a reward for what they have done.

What joy it will be to hear Him say, *"Well done, good and faithful servant"* (Matthew 25:23)! You who have worked for Christ when nobody else knew will find that Christ took stock of it all. You who served the Lord while being slandered will find that the Lord Jesus cleared the chaff away from the wheat and knew that you were one of His precious ones. What bliss you will know when He says, *"Enter thou into the joy of thy lord"* (Matthew 25:21).

But, how terrible for the ungodly it will be! They are to receive the things that they have done, that is to say, the due punishment. Not every man will receive the same punishment: to the greater sinner, the greater doom; to the man who sinned against light, a greater damnation than to the man who did not have the same light. Sodom and Gomorrah will receive their place; Tyre and Sidon theirs; and then to Capernaum and Bethsaida their place of more intolerable torment, because they had the Gospel and rejected it. So the Holy Spirit tells us: *"For we must all appear before the judgment seat of Christ; that every one may receive the things done in his body, according to that he hath done, whether it be good or bad."*

Not only will the punishment be meted out in proportion to the transgression, but the consequences to be endured will also be a development of the evil actions done, for every man *"shall...eat the fruit of* [his] *own way"* (Proverbs 1:31). Sin, in the natural order, ripens into sorrow. This is not blind fate but the operation of a divine law, wise and invariable.

How dreadful it will be for the malicious man to gnaw forever on his own envious heart, to find his malice coming back home to him as a bird comes home to roost, to hoot forever in his own soul! How torturous it will be for the lustful man to feel, burning in every vein, lust that he can never gratify; for the drunkard to have a thirst that not even a sea of water could quench, if he could find any water; for the glutton who has fared sumptuously to be perpetually hungry; for the wrathful person to be forever raging, with the fire of anger burning like a volcano in his soul; and for the rebel against God to be forever defiant, cursing God whom he cannot touch and finding his curses coming back on himself.

There is no punishment worse than for a man who is sinfully disposed to gratify his lusts, to satiate his bad propensities, and to multiply and fatten his vices. Let men grow into what they would be, and then see what they have become! Take away the policemen in some parts of London; give the people plenty of money; let them do just as they please; and watch what happens.

For example, recently, at least six men got broken heads in a street brawl, and their wives and children were in one general skirmish. If those people were to be kept together while their vigor continued unimpaired by age or decay and their characters kept on developing, they would act worse than a pack of wolves. Let them give way to their rage and anger, with nothing to check their passions. Let miserly, greedy people go on forever with their greed. It makes them miserable here, but let these things be indulged in forever, and what worse hell could there be? Oh, sin is hell, and holiness is heaven!

Men will receive the things done in their bodies. If God has graced them with love for Him, they will continue loving Him. If God has given them trust for Him, they will keep on trusting Him. If God has made them to be like Christ, they will go on being Christlike, and they will receive, as a reward, the things done in their bodies.

However, if a man has lived in sin, *"he which is filthy, let him be filthy still"* (Revelation 22:11). He who was unbelieving will continue to be unbelieving. The damnation of unrepentant sinners, then, will be *"where their worm dieth not, and the fire is not quenched"* (Mark 9:44), to which will be added the wrath of God forever and ever.

May every one of us be given the grace to flee to Christ, for in Him is our only safety. Simple faith in Jesus is the true basis for the character that will produce the evidence that you are chosen by God. A simple belief in the merits of the Lord Jesus, brought about in us by the Holy Spirit, is the solid rock upon which will be built, by the same divine Builder, the character that will establish the truth that the kingdom was prepared for us from before the foundations of the world. May God form such a character in each of us, for Christ's sake. Amen.

Chapter Five

Jesus Glorified in His Saints

*When he shall come to be glorified in his saints,
and to be admired in all them that believe
(because our testimony among you
was believed) in that day.*
—2 Thessalonians 1:10

What a difference between the first and second comings of our Lord! When Christ comes a second time, it will be to be glorified and admired, but when He came the first time, it was to be *"despised and rejected of men"* (Isaiah 53:3). He is coming a second time to reign with unparalleled splendor, but the first time He came to die in circumstances of shame and sorrow.

139

Lift up your eyes, you who have received His light, and anticipate the change that will be as great for you as for your Lord. Now you are hidden, even as He was hidden, and misunderstood, even as He was misunderstood, when He walked among the sons of men. *"We know that, when he shall appear, we shall be like him; for we shall see him as he is"* (1 John 3:2). His manifestation will be our manifestation. In that Last Day, when He will be revealed in glory, His saints will be glorified with Him.

In the verses just prior to our text, observe that our Lord is spoken of as follows:

> [7] *And to you who are troubled rest with us, when the Lord Jesus shall be revealed from heaven with his mighty angels,*
> [8] *In flaming fire taking vengeance on them that know not God, and that obey not the gospel of our Lord Jesus Christ.*
>
> (2 Thessalonians 1:7–8)

Christ will come in His glory and, at the same time, He will take vengeance in flaming fire on those who do not know God and who do not obey the Gospel. This should be a note of great terror to all those who are ignorant of God and are wickedly unbelieving concerning Christ. Let them take heed, for the Lord will gain glory by the overthrow of His enemies. Those who would not bow before Him cheerfully will be compelled to bow before Him abjectly. They will crouch at His feet; they will lick the dust in terror; and at the glance of His eyes, they will utterly wither away. As it is written, they *"shall be punished with everlasting destruction from the presence of the Lord, and from the glory of his power"* (2 Thessalonians 1:9).

However, this is not the main reason for which Christ will come, nor is this the matter in which He will find His chief glory. Observe that He does this almost as an aside, when He is coming for another purpose. To destroy the wicked is a matter of necessity in which He takes no delight. According to the whole context, He does this, not because He is coming for that purpose, but as He is returning to the earth *"to be glorified in his saints, and to be admired in them that believe."*

The crowning honor of Christ will be seen in His people. This is the purpose for which He will return to the earth in the latter days, so that He may be exceedingly magnified in His saints. Even now, however, His saints glorify Him. When they walk in holiness, they reflect His light, as it were. Their holy deeds are beams from Him who is *"the Sun of righteousness"* (Malachi 4:2). When they believe in Him, they also glorify Him, for there is no grace that pays more respectful and deeper homage to our Lord than the grace of faith by which we trust Him and so confess Him to be our all in all.

Yes, we do glorify our gracious Lord, but, beloved, we must all confess that we do not do this as we desire. Alas, too often we dishonor Him and grieve the Holy Spirit. By our lack of zeal and by our many sins, we are guilty of discrediting His Gospel and dishonoring His name. Happy will be the time when this will no more be possible. Then we will be rid of the inward corruption that now works itself into outward sin. Then we will never dishonor Christ again. Then we will shine with a clear, pure radiance, as did the moon on the first Passover night, when she looked the sun full in the face and then shone her best on the earth.

Today we are pottery vessels on the wheel. Even though we are now only half fashioned, some of His divine skill can still be seen in us as His handiwork. But, the molded clay is only seen in part, and much remains to be done. How much more of the great Potter's creative wisdom and sanctifying power will be displayed when we are the perfect products of His hand! In the unfolding bud, the new nature brings honor to its Author; it will do far more when its perfection manifests the Finisher. When the days of the new creation are ended and

God ushers in the eternal rest by pronouncing His work of grace to be very good, then Jesus will be glorified and admired in all of us.

As God helps me, I first want to address the special glorification of Christ referred to in our text. Secondly, I desire to call your attention to the special considerations that this grand truth suggests.

The Special Glorification of Christ

Let us consider carefully what is entailed in this special glorification of our Lord: *"When he shall come to be glorified in his saints, and to be admired in all them that believe (because our testimony among you was believed) in that day."*

When Christ Will Be Glorified

The first point to note is the time. Our text says, *"When he shall come to be glorified in his saints...in that day."* The full glorification of Christ in His saints will occur when He comes the second time, according to the sure word of prophecy. Yes, He is glorified in them at present, for He said, *"All mine are thine, and thine are mine; and I am glorified in them"* (John 17:10). However, as of now, that glory is perceptible to Him rather than to the outside world.

The lamps are being trimmed. (See Matthew 25:1–13.) They will shine before long. These are the days of preparation before that revered moment that will be a high holy Day in an infinite sense. As Esther prepared and purified herself with myrrh and sweet perfumes for so many months (Esther 2:12) before she entered the king's palace to be espoused to him, so are we now being purified and made ready for that Day when the perfected church will be presented to Christ as a bride is presented to her husband. We will be *"prepared as a bride adorned for her husband"* (Revelation 21:2).

This is our night in which we must watch, but the morning is coming, a morning without clouds. Then we will walk in a sevenfold light because our Well Beloved has come. His Second Advent will be His revelation. He was under a cloud when He was here before: except for a few who *"beheld his glory"* (John 1:14), men perceived Him not (Luke 24:16). But, when He comes a second time, all veils will be removed, and *"every eye shall see"* (Revelation 1:7) the glory of His countenance.

For this He waits, and His church waits with Him. We do not know when that time will arrive, but every hour is bringing it nearer to us. Therefore, let us stand, *"looking for and* [eagerly awaiting] *the coming of the day of God"* (2 Peter 3:12).

In Whom Glorified

Note, secondly, in whom this glorification of Christ is to be found. The text does not say He will be glorified "by" His saints, but *"in his saints."* There is more than a slight shade of difference between those two terms. We endeavor to glorify Christ now by our actions, but when He returns, we will glorify Him in our persons, characters, and conditions. At present, He is glorified by what we do, but at His future coming, He will be glorified in what we are.

Who are these people in whom Jesus is to be glorified and admired? They are spoken of with two descriptions: *"in his saints"* and *"in all them that believe."* First, let us explore *"in his saints."* All those in whom Christ will be glorified are described as holy ones or saints: men and women who have been sanctified and made pure; those whose gracious lives show that they have been under the teaching of the Holy Spirit; those whose obedient actions prove that they are disciples of a Holy Master, even of Him who was *"holy, harmless, undefiled, separate from sinners"* (Hebrews 7:26).

145

Inasmuch as these saints are also said to be believers, I gather that the holiness that will honor Christ at the Last Day is a holiness based on faith in Him. The root of their holiness is that they first trusted in Christ, and then, being saved, they loved their Lord and obeyed Him. Their faith, brought about by His love, purified their souls, and thus cleansed their lives. It is an inner purity as well as an outward chastity, arising out of the living and operative principle of faith.

If some people think they can attain holiness apart from faith in Christ, they are as mistaken as the person who hopes to reap a harvest without first sowing seed into the furrows. Faith is the bulb, and sainthood is the delightfully fragrant flower that comes from it when it is planted in the soil of a renewed heart.

Beware, I urge you, of any pretense of holiness arising out of yourselves and maintained by the energy of your own unaided wills. You might as well try to gather grapes from thorns or figs from thistles. (See Matthew 7:16.) True sainthood must spring from confidence in the Savior of sinners. If it does not, it is lacking in the first element of truth. How can anyone have a perfect character who finds his basis for it in self-esteem? How could Christ be glorified by saints who refuse to trust in Him?

I call your attention once again to the second description, *"all them that believe."* This is emphasized by the hint that they are believers in a particular testimony, according to the parenthetical clause, *"because our testimony among you was believed."* Now, the testimony of the apostles concerned what they had witnessed of Jesus. They saw Him in the body, and they bore witness that He was God *"manifest in the flesh"* (1 Timothy 3:16). They saw His holy life and attested to it. They saw His grievous death, and they testified that *"God was in Christ, reconciling the world unto himself"* (2 Corinthians 5:19). They saw Him risen from the dead, and they said, "We are witnesses of His resurrection." (See Acts 1:22.) They saw Him rise into heaven, and they bore witness that God had taken Him up to His right hand.

All who believe this witness are saved. *"If thou shalt confess with thy mouth the Lord Jesus, and shalt believe in thine heart that God hath raised him from the dead, thou shalt be saved"* (Romans 10:9). All who, with simple faith, come and cast themselves upon the incarnate Son of God, who died and rose again for men and *"who is even at the right hand of God, who also maketh intercession for us"* (Romans 8:34)—these are the ones in whom Christ will be glorified and admired.

However, since they are first said to be saints, let it never be forgotten that this must be a living faith, a faith that produces a hatred of sin, a faith that renews the character and shapes the life after the noble model of Christ, thus turning sinners into saints. The two descriptions must not be violently torn apart. You must not say that the favored people are sanctified without remembering that they are justified by faith. Neither should you say that they are justified by faith without remembering that without *"holiness...no man shall see the Lord"* (Hebrews 12:14), and that, in the end, the people in whom Christ will be admired will be those holy ones who were saved by faith in Him.

By Whom Glorified

So far, then, we are clear, but now a question arises: By whom will Christ be glorified and admired? First of all, I answer that His people will personally do so. Every saint will glorify Christ in himself and admire Christ in himself. Each one will marvel, "What a wonder that a poor creature such as I am should be thus perfected! How glorious is my Lord, who has worked this miracle in me!" Surely our consciousness of having been cleansed and made holy will cause us to fulfill those words of John Berridge:

> He cheers them with eternal smile,
> They sing hosannas all the while;
> Or, overwhelm'd with rapture sweet,
> Sink down adoring at His feet.

This I know, that when I personally enter heaven, I will forever admire and adore the everlasting love that brought me there. Yes, we will all glorify and admire our Savior for what He has done in us personally by His infinite grace.

The saints will also admire Christ in one another. When I see you and you see your brothers and sisters in Christ all perfect, we will be filled with wonder and gratitude and delight. You will be free from all envy there, and therefore you will rejoice in all the beauty of your fellow saints. Their heaven will be a heaven to you, and what a multitude of heavens you will have as you rejoice in the joy of all the redeemed! We will as much admire the Lord's handiwork in others as in ourselves, and each one will praise Him for saving all the rest. You will see your Lord in all your brothers and sisters, and this will make you praise and adore Him, world without end, with a perpetual amazement of ever growing delight.

However, that will not be all. Besides the blood-bought and ransomed of Christ, there will be at His Coming all the holy angels, who will stand by and look on with wonder. They greatly marveled when first He stooped from heaven to the earth, and they desired to look into those things that then were a mystery to them. (See 1 Peter 1:12.) But, when they see their beloved Prince come back with ten thousand times ten thousand of the ransomed at His feet, all of them made perfect by having *"washed their robes, and made them white in the blood of the Lamb"* (Revelation 7:14), how the heavenly beings will admire Him in every one of His redeemed! How they will praise that conquering arm that has brought home all these spoils from the war! How the hosts of heaven will shout His praises as they see Him lead these captives captive with a new captivity (see Ephesians 4:8), in chains of love, joyfully gracing His triumph and showing forth the completeness of His victory!

We do not know what other races of creatures there may be, but I think it is no stretch of the imagination to believe that, as this world is only one speck in the creation of God, there may be millions of other races in the countless worlds around us, and all of these may be invited to behold the wonders of redeeming love as manifested in the saints in the Day of the Lord. I seem to see these other intelligences encompassing the saints as *"a cloud of witnesses"* (Hebrews 12:1), and in rapt attention, beholding in them the love and grace of the redeeming Lord. What songs, what shouts, what hymns, will rise from all these to the praise of the eternal God! What an orchestra of praise the universe will become! From star to star the holy melodies will roll, until all space will ring out the hosannas of wondering spirits. *"Wonderful, Counsellor, The mighty God, The everlasting Father, The Prince of Peace"* (Isaiah 9:6), will have brought home all those who are inspiring such wondrous joy, and they with Himself will be the wonder of eternity.

Then Satan and his defeated legions, along with the lost spirits of ungodly men, will bite their lips with envy and rage and tremble at the majesty of Jesus in that Day. By their confessed defeat and manifest despair, they will glorify Him in His people, in whom they have been utterly overthrown. They will see that there is not one lost whom He redeemed by His blood, not one snatched away of all the sheep His Father gave Him (see John 10:27–30), not one warrior enlisted beneath His banner who fell in battle, but all are *"more than conquerors through him that loved* [them]" (Romans 8:37).

What despair will seize upon diabolic spirits as they discover their entire defeat—defeated in men who were once their slaves! Poor dupes whom they could so easily beguile by their craftiness—defeated even in these! Jesus, triumphant by taking the lambs from between the lion's jaws and rescuing His feeble sheep from their power, will utterly put them to shame in His redeemed. With what anguish they will sink into the hell prepared for them, because now they hear with anger all the earth and heaven and every star ringing with the shout, *"Alleluia: for the Lord God omnipotent reigneth"* (Revelation 19:6), and, "The Lamb has conquered by His blood."

To What Degree Glorified

Since we now know there will be enough spectators to magnify Christ in His saints, let us inquire, To what degree will the Lord Jesus be glorified? My answer is that it will be to the very highest degree. He will come to be glorified in His saints to the utmost, for this is clear from the words, *"to be admired."* When this translation was made, the word *admire* had, to ordinary Englishmen, a stronger inference of wonder than it has now. We often speak of admiring a thing in the less intense sense of liking or desiring it, but the real meaning of the English word, and of the Greek also, is "wonder." Our Lord will be wondered at *"in all them that believe."* Those who look upon the saints will suddenly be struck with a feeling of sacred delight and awe. They will be startled with the surprising glory of the Lord's work in them. "We thought He could do great things, but this—this surpasses conception!"

Every saint will be a wonder to himself. "I thought my bliss would be great, but not like this!" All his brothers and sisters will be a startling wonder to the perfected believer. He will exclaim, "I thought the saints would be perfect, but I never imagined that such an excessive transformation of glory would be put upon each of us. I could not have dreamed my Lord would be so good and gracious to His feeble followers."

The angels in heaven will say that they never anticipated such deeds of grace. They knew that He had undertaken a great work, but they did not realize that He would do so much for and in His people. The firstborn sons of light, accustomed to seeing great marvels performed in ancient times, will be entranced with a new, unsurpassed wonder as they see the handiwork of Immanuel's free grace and dying love.

The men who once despised the saints, who called them pious hypocrites and trampled on them (perhaps having slayed them), the kings and princes of the earth who sold the righteous for a pair of shoes, what will they say when they see the lowliest of the Savior's followers become a prince of more illustrious rank than the greatest ones of the world, and Christ shining out in all of these favored beings? For their uplifting, Jesus Christ will be wondered at by those who once despised both Him and them.

In What Ways Glorified

The next question leads us into the very heart of the subject: In what ways will Christ be glorified and wondered at? Do not expect me to cover one tenth of it, for I am unable to do so. I am only going to give you a little sample of what this must mean. Exhaustive exposition is quite impossible for me.

With regard to His saints, I think that Jesus will be glorified and wondered at by virtue of their number: *"a great multitude, which no man could number"* (Revelation 7:9). The apostle John was a great mathematician, and he managed to count up to one hundred and forty-four thousand (Revelation 14:1) of all the tribes of the children of Israel, but that was only a representative member for the Jewish nation. As for the church of God, comprised of the Gentile nations, he gave up all idea of computation and confessed that he saw *"a great multitude, which no man could number."* When the Beloved Apostle heard them sing, he said, *"I heard a voice from heaven, as the voice of many waters, and as the voice of a great thunder"* (Revelation 14:2). There were so many of them that their song was as the Mediterranean Sea whipped to a fury by a tempest—no, not one great sea in an uproar, but ocean upon ocean, the Atlantic and the Pacific piled upon each other, and the Arctic on these, and other oceans on these, layers of oceans, all thundering out their mightiest roar. Such will be the song of the redeemed, for the crowds that swell the unparalleled hymn will be beyond all reckoning.

You who laughed at His kingdom, behold and see how the One has become thousands! Now look, you foes of Christ, and see the fulfillment of that prophecy, long ago foretold:

[16] *There shall be an handful of corn in the earth upon the top of the mountains; the fruit thereof shall shake like Lebanon: and they of the city shall flourish like grass of the earth.* (Psalm 72:16)

Who can number the drops of the dew or the sands on the seashore? When he has counted these, still he will not have guessed at the multitude of the redeemed that Christ will bring to glory.

All this harvest will have come from one grain of wheat, which would have remained alone had it not fallen to the ground and died. What did the Word say? *"If it die, it bringeth forth much fruit"* (John 12:24). Was this prophecy not fulfilled? O beloved, what a harvest from the solitary Man of Nazareth! What fruit from that glorious Branch!

Men *"did esteem him stricken, smitten of God and afflicted"* (Isaiah 53:4). Even though men made nothing of Jesus, there still sprang from Him these multitudes that are as many as the stars of heaven. Is He not glorified and wondered at in His saints? The Judgment Day will declare it without fail.

However, there is quality as well as quantity that will draw such glory and admiration. Christ will be admired in His saints because they are, each one of them, proof of His power to save from evil. My eye can hardly bear, even though it is only in my imagination, to gaze on the glittering ranks of the white-robed ones, as each one outshines the sun and all are as if a magnified midday had clothed them. Yet all these, as I look at them, tell me, "We have washed our robes, for they were once defiled. We have made them white, but this whiteness is caused by the blood of the Lamb." (See Revelation 7:14.)

They were *"by nature the children of wrath, even as others"* (Ephesians 2:3). They were *"dead in trespasses and sins"* (Ephesians 2:1). *"All we like sheep have gone astray; we have turned every one to his own way"* (Isaiah 53:6). Yet, look at them, and see how He has saved them, washed them, cleansed them, perfected them! His power and grace are seen in all of them. If your eyes pause here and there, you will discover some that were supremely stubborn, whose necks were like iron sinews, and still He conquered them by love. Some were densely ignorant, but He opened their blind eyes. Some were grossly infected with the leprosy of lust, but He healed them.

Some were under Satan's most terrible power, but He cast the Devil out of them. Oh, how Christ will be glorified in special cases! That drunkard has been transformed into a saint. This blasphemer has been turned into a loving disciple. That persecutor, who radiated threats of torture, has been taught to sing a hymn of praise forever! The Lord will be extremely glorified in them.

Beloved in the Lord, in each one of us there was some special difficulty as to our salvation, some impossibility that was possible with God, though it would have been forever impossible with us (Mark 10:27). Thus, Christ will be glorified forever in each of us because He overcame those impossible obstacles in us to bring us unto Himself.

Remember, also, that all those saints made perfect would have been in hell had it not been for the Son's atoning sacrifice. They will remember this most vividly, because they will see other men condemned for the sins with which they also were once polluted. The crush of vengeance upon the ungodly will make the saints magnify the Lord all the more as they see themselves delivered. They will each feel,

> Oh, were it not for grace divine,
> That fate so dreadful had been mine.

In all of the saints, the memory of the horrible pit from which they were drawn and the miry clay out of which they were lifted will make their Savior more glorious and wonderful.

Perhaps the principal point in which Christ will be glorified will be the absolute perfection of all the saints. They will then be without *"spot, or wrinkle, or any such thing"* (Ephesians 5:27). We have not experienced what perfection is, and therefore we can hardly conceive it. Our thoughts themselves are too sinful for us to get a full idea of what absolute perfection must be. But, dear friends, we will have no sin left in us, for we will be *"without fault before the throne of God"* (Revelation 14:5). We will have no remaining propensity to sin. There will be no bias in the flesh toward that which is evil, but our whole beings will be fixed forever upon that which is good. The affections will never be wanton again; instead, they will always be chaste for Christ. The understanding will never make mistakes. We will never again *"put bitter for sweet, and sweet for bitter!"* (Isaiah 5:20). We will be *"perfect, even as* [our] *Father which is in heaven is perfect"* (Matthew 5:48).

Truly, beloved, He who works this in us will be a wonder. Christ will be admired and adored because of this grand result. O mighty Master, with what strange moral alchemy did You work to turn that morosely dispositioned man into a mass of love! How did You work to lift that selfish lover of mammon up from his hoarded gains to make him find his gain in You? How did You overcome that proud spirit, that fickle spirit, that lazy spirit, that lustful spirit—how did You contrive to take all these away? How did You exterminate the roots of

sin, even the fine root hairs, out of Your redeemed, so that not one tiny filament remains?

> [20] *In those days, and in that time, saith the*
> *LORD, the iniquity of Israel shall be sought*
> *for, and there shall be none; and the sins of*
> *Judah, and they shall not be found: for I*
> *will pardon them whom I reserve.*
>
> (Jeremiah 50:20)

Neither the guilt of sin nor the propensity
to sin will exist—both will be completely
eliminated from His saints. Christ will have
done it, and He thus will be *"glorified in his*
saints, and... admired in them that believe."

This is but the beginning, however. In that
wondrous Day, in all of the saints will be seen
the wisdom and power and love of Christ in
having brought them through every trial of the
way. He kept their faith alive when it otherwise would have died out. He sustained them
under trials when they would have fainted. He
held them fast in their integrity when temptation solicited them and their feet almost
slipped. He sustained some of them in prison,
on the rack, and at the stake, and He held
them faithful still!

One might hardly wish to be a martyr, but
I think that the martyrs will be the admiration
of us all, or rather Christ will be admired in

them greatly. How they could bear such pain as some of them endured for Christ's sake none of us can guess, except that we know that Christ was in them, suffering in His members. Jesus will eternally be wondered at in them as all intelligent spirits see how He upheld them, so that *"tribulation, or distress, or persecution, or famine, or nakedness, or peril, or sword"* (Romans 8:35) could not separate them from His love. These were the faithful who *"wandered about in sheepskins and goatskins; being destitute, afflicted, tormented; (of whom the world was not worthy)"* (Hebrews 11:37–38). However, now arrayed as kings and priests, they stand in surpassing glory forever. Truly, the Lord will be admired in them.

Recollect, dear friends, that we will see in that Day how the blessed Christ, as *"the head over all things"* (Ephesians 1:22), has governed every providence for the sanctification of His people: how the dark days brought showers that made the plants of the Lord grow, how the fierce sun that threatened to scorch them to the root filled them with the warmth of love divine and ripened their choice fruit.

What a tale the saints will have to tell of how that which tried to dampen the fire of grace made it burn more mightily, how the stone that threatened to kill their faith was turned into bread for them, how the rod and staff of the Good Shepherd were ever with them to bring them safely home. I have sometimes thought that if I get into heaven by the skin of my teeth, I will sit down on heaven's shore and forever bless Him who, on a board or on a broken piece of the ship, brought my soul safely to land. Surely they who obtain an abundant entrance, coming into the fair havens like a ship in full sail without danger of shipwreck, will have to praise the Lord that they thus came into the blessed port of peace. In each case the Lord will be especially glorified and admired.

I cannot linger over this, but I beg you to notice that, as a king is glorious in his regalia, so Christ will put on His saints as His personal splendor in that Day when He takes up His jewels. It will be with Christ as it was with a virtuous matron of nobility who, when she called at her friends' homes and saw their baubles, asked them to come the next day to her home so she could exhibit her jewels. They expected to see rubies and pearls and diamonds, but she called in her two boys and said, "These are my jewels." Likewise, Jesus will exhibit His saints instead of emerald and amethyst, onyx and topaz. "These are my choice treasures," He will say, "in whom I am glorified."

Solomon surely was never more full of glory than when he had finished the temple, when all the tribes came together to see the noble structure and confessed it to be *"beautiful for situation, the joy of the whole earth"* (Psalm 48:2). But, what glory Christ will have when all the living stones are put into their places and His church has her agate windows, her carbuncle gates, and all her borders of precious stones! Then, indeed, will He be glorified, when the foundations of His New Jerusalem are courses of stones most precious, the likes of which have never been seen before.

In Believers

Inasmuch as our text puts special emphasis on believing, *"in all them that believe,"* I invite you to consider how, as believers as well as saints, the raised ones will glorify their Lord.

First, it will be wonderful that there are so many from varied walks of life brought to faith in Him: men with no God and men with many gods, men steeped in ignorance and men puffed up with carnal wisdom, great men and poor men, all brought to believe in the one Redeemer and to praise Him for His great salvation. Will He not be glorified in their common faith? It will magnify Him that these will all be saved by faith and not by their own merits. Not one among them will boast that he was saved by his own good works, but all will rejoice to have been saved by that blessedly simple way of "Believe and live," and by sovereign grace through the atoning blood, looked to by the tearful eyes of pure faith.

This, too, will make Jesus glorious: all of them, weak as they were, were made strong by faith; and all of them, as personally unfit for battle as they were, were still made triumphant in conflict because, by faith, they overcame through the blood of the Lamb (Revelation 12:11). All of them will be there to show that their faith was honored, that Christ was faithful to His promise, and that He never allowed them to believe in vain. All of them, standing in heavenly places, saved by faith, will ascribe every particle of the glory only to the Lord Jesus:

> I ask them whence their victory came?
> They, with united breath
> Ascribe their conquest to the Lamb,
> Their triumph to His death.

They believed and were saved, but faith takes no credit for itself. It is a self-denying grace and puts the crown upon the head of Christ. Therefore, it is written that He will *"be glorified in his saints, and* [also] *be admired in all them that believe."*

In Resurrected Bodies

Next, I would like you to reflect that Jesus will be glorified in the risen bodies of all His saints. Those who have died and are in heaven are pure spirits in their present state, but when He returns, they will be clothed again. Poor body, you must sleep awhile, but what you will be at your awakening does not yet appear. (See 1 John 3:1.) You are now the shriveled seed, but there is a flower to come from you that will be lovely beyond all thought. Though sown in weakness, this body will be raised in power. Though *"sown in corruption; it is raised in incorruption"* (1 Corinthians 15:42).

Weakness, sickness, pain, and death will be banished forever. Infirmity and deformity will be completely unknown. The Lord will raise us up with glorious, eternal bodies:

[52] *For the trumpet shall sound, and the dead shall be raised incorruptible, and we shall be changed.*
[53] *For this corruptible must put on incorruption, and this mortal must put on immortality.* (1 Corinthians 15:53)

> [2] *Beloved, now are we the sons of God, and it doth not yet appear what we shall be: but we know that, when he shall appear, we shall be like him; for we shall see him as he is.* (1 John 3:2)

Oh, what a prospect lies before us! Let us remember that this blessed resurrection will come to us because He rose from the dead, for there must be a resurrection to the members because the Head has risen. Oh, the delight of being a risen man, perfect in body, soul, and spirit! All that beauty will be due to Christ, and therefore He will be admired in us.

In All Who Believe

Next, let us consider the absolute perfection of the church regarding its numbers. All who have believed in Christ will be with Him in glory. Notice the word *all* in our text, which says Christ will be *"admired in all them that believe."* If some of those who have believed in Him somehow perished, He could not be admired in them. But, they will all be there, the little ones as well as the great ones.

You will be there, you poor feeble folk who, when you say, *"Lord, I believe,"* are obliged to add, *"help thou mine unbelief"* (Mark 9:24). He will be admired in all believers, without a single exception. Possibly there will be more wonder at the weak believers going to heaven than at the stronger ones. Mr. Greatheart, when he comes there, will owe his victories to his Master and lay his laurels at Christ's feet. But, when fainting Feeblemind, limping Ready-to-halt with his crutches, and trembling Little-faith enter into rest, they will make heaven ring with notes of even greater admiration because such poor, creeping worms of the earth have won the day by mighty grace.

Suppose that one of them were missing at the Last Great Day. Stop the harps! Silence the songs! There will be no beginning to be merry while one child is shut out. I am quite certain that if, as an earthly family, we were going to sing our evening hymn of joy and thankfulness, but mother said, "Where is the little mite? Where is the baby of the family?" we would pause. If we had to say that the baby was lost, there would be no singing and no resting until she had been found.

It is the glory of Jesus that, as our Shepherd, He has lost none of His flock, and, as the Captain of Salvation, He has brought many sons to glory and has lost none. Hence, He is admired, not in some that believe, nor yet in all but one, but He is *admired in all them that believe.*

Does this not bring you delight, you who are weak and trembling, that Christ will be admired in you? There is little to admire in you at present, as you penitently confess. But, since Christ is in you now, and will be more fully manifested in you, before long there will be much to admire. May you partake in the excellence of our divine Lord and be conformed to His likeness so that He may be seen and glorified in you.

In Eternal Safety

Another point of admiration will be the eternal safety of all His believing people. There they are safe from fear of harm. You dogs of hell, you howled at their heels and hoped to devour them, but they have deftly escaped from you! What must it be like to be lifted out of range of the Enemy's weapons, where no more guard needs to be kept, for even the roar of the satanic canons cannot be heard? O glorious Christ, to bring them all to such a state of safety, You are to be wondered at forever.

In Reflected Glory

Moreover, all the saints will be so honored, so happy, and so like their Lord that they themselves and everything about them will be themes for endless admiration.

You may have seen a room decorated with mirrors hung all around the walls. When you stood in the middle, you were reflected from every point. You were seen here, and there, and there again, and there once more, so that every part of you was reflected. Heaven will be just like that, with Jesus at the center and all His saints reflecting His glory like mirrors. Is He human? So are they. Is He the Son of God? So are they sons of God. Is He perfect? So are they. Is He exalted? So are they. Is He a prophet? So are they, making known *"unto the principalities and powers in heavenly places …the manifold wisdom of God"* (Ephesians 3:10). Is He a priest? So are they. Is He the King? So are they, for He *"hath made us kings and priests unto God"* (Revelation 1:6), and we will reign forever and ever. Look where you might among the ranks of the redeemed, this one thing will be seen: the glory of Christ Jesus, even to your surprise and wonder.

Practical Applications

I have limited space to draw out the text's functional implications, so I will just tell you what they are without much explanation.

Take Stock

First of all, our text suggests that each of us should conduct a self-examination and that the principal subject for this introspection should be: Am I a saint? Am I holy? Am I a believer in Christ? Now is the time for you to determine whether your answer is yes or no, for on your true word depends your eternal glorification of Christ or your banishment from His presence forever.

Expect Reproach

The next thing we can derive is the small value of human opinion. When Christ was here, the world reckoned Him to be a nobody; while His people are here, they must expect to be judged in the same way. What do worldlings know about it? How soon their petty judgments will be reversed! When our Lord next appears, even those who sneered will be compelled to admire. When they see the glory of Christ in His people, they will be awestricken and will have nothing to say against us—not even the false tongue of malicious slander will dare to hiss out one serpent word in the end. Never mind them, then. Just put up with the reproach that will soon be silenced.

An Encouragement to Sinners

The next suggestion is a great encouragement to inquirers who are seeking Christ. I am specifically urging you, you great sinners, to ponder this: If Jesus is to be glorified in saved sinners, would He not be glorified indeed if He saved you? If He were ever to save such a rebel as you have been, would it not be the astonishment of eternity? You who are known in your neighborhood as wicked Jack or as a common thief, what if my Master were to make a saint of you? Of course, you are bad raw material! Yet, suppose He transformed you into a precious jewel and made you to be as holy as God is holy, what would you say of Him?

"Say of Him?" you reply. "I would praise Him, world without end." Yes, and you will do so if you will come and trust Him. Just put your trust in Him. May the Lord help you to do so at once, and He will be admired even in you forever and ever.

Love One Another

Our text also gives an exhortation to believers. Will Jesus Christ be honored and glorified in all the saints? Then, let us think well of them all and love them all. Some dear children of God do not have beautiful looks, or they are blind or deformed or maimed. Many of them have scanty wallets, and it may be that the church knows most of them from when they come for alms. Moreover, they may have little intellect and little power to please; they may be uncouth in their manners; they belong to what are called the lowest ranks of society. Do not despise them because of these things, for soon our Lord will be glorified in them.

How Christ will be admired in that poor, bedridden woman when she rises from her ghetto cot to sing hallelujah to God and the Lamb, along with the brightest of the shining ones! Why, I think the pain, the poverty, the weakness, and the sorrow of saints below will greatly glorify the Captain of their Salvation as they tell how grace helped them to bear their burdens and to rejoice while enduring their afflictions.

Share Your Testimony

Finally, beloved, this text ought to encourage all of you who love Jesus to go on talking about Him to others and bearing your testimony for His name. You see how the apostle Paul has inserted a few words by way of parentheses. Draw the words out of the brackets, and take them to heart: *"Because our testimony among you was believed."*

Do you see those crowds of idolatrous heathen, and do you see those hosts of saved ones before the throne? What was the medium that linked the two groups? By what visible means did those sinners become saints? Do you see that insignificant-looking man with the weak eyes, that man whose bodily presence is puny and whose speech is contemptible? Do you see his needle case and his sewing instruments? He has been making and mending tents, for he is only a tentmaker.

Now, those bright spirits that shine like suns, beaming forth with the rays of Christ's glory, were made so bright through the addresses and prayers of that tentmaker. The Thessalonians were heathens plunged in sin, and this poor tentmaker came in among them and told them of Jesus Christ and His Gospel. They believed his testimony. That belief changed the lives of his hearers and made them holy. Being renewed, they came at length to be perfected in holiness. Thus they became, and Jesus Christ is glorified in them.

Beloved, it will be a delightful thing throughout eternity to contemplate that you went into your Sunday school class, afraid you could not say much, but you talked about Jesus

Christ with a tear in your eye, and you brought a dear girl to believe in His saving name through your testimony. In years to come, that girl will be among those that shine out to the glory of Christ forever. Perhaps you will get a chance to talk in a mission to some of those poor, despised tramps. Maybe you will tell one of those poor vagrants or one of the fallen women the story of your Lord's love and blood. Just possibly, the poor broken heart will latch onto the gracious word and come to Jesus. Then a heavenly character will have begun and another jewel will have been secured for the Redeemer's diadem.

I think that you will admire His crown all the more because, as you see certain stones sparkling in it, you will say, "Blessed be His name forever. He helped me to dive into the sea and find that pearl for Him, and now it adorns His sacred brow."

Now, get at it, all of you! You who are doing nothing for Jesus, be ashamed of yourselves, and ask Him to work in you that you may begin to work for Him. Unto God be the glory, forever and ever. Amen.